Fate of a Cockroach

A Three Continents Book

Fate of a Cockroach and Other Plays

Tawfiq al-Hakim

translated from the Arabic
by Denys Johnson-Davies

LYNNE
RIENNER
PUBLISHERS

BOULDER
LONDON

Published in the United States of America in 1996 by
Lynne Rienner Publishers, Inc.
1800 30th Street, Boulder, Colorado 80301
www.rienner.com

and in the United Kingdom by
Lynne Rienner Publishers, Inc.
3 Henrietta Street, Covent Garden, London WC2E 8LU

First published in 1980 by Three Continents Press.

ISBN 0-89410-197-8 (pbk. : alk. paper)

Printed and bound in the United States of America

5   4   3

Contents

Introduction

Born in 1902 in Alexandria, Tewfik Al Hakim has occupied a
central place in the Arab literary scene since he first made a name
for himself in the late 'twenties. He is known primarily as a
playwright, with an output of some seventy plays, and one of
Cairo's theatres has been named after him. He has also
produced several volumes of essays, a few short stories, and some
enjoyable volumes of autobiography; at least two of his novels are
landmarks in modern Arabic literature.

Tewfik Al Hakim became interested in the theatre at an early
age. At that time, however, it offered neither a respectable nor a
reliable means of livelihood and it is not surprising that his upper
middle class parents showed no enthusiasm for his literary
ambitions; in his autobiography he records how he did not allow
his full name to appear on one of his early plays for fear that the
news that he was the author might reach his parents. He was
therefore persuaded to study law, which he did initially in Cairo.
Having taken his degree, he was sent to Paris to complete his
legal studies. He stayed in Paris from 1925 until 1928, where he
spent the greater part of his time in the company of writers and
many of his evenings at the theatre; he also read widely in
French. On his return to Egypt he was appointed an attorney
to the Public Prosecutor in the provinces and his experiences
there provided the material for his novel *The Maze of Justice*.* It
was not long before he resigned from government service and
devoted himself wholly to creative writing. Since then he has held
a number of official appointments, including that of Director of
the National Library in Cairo; he has also been his country's
permanent representative with UNESCO in Paris.

*The translation of this early novel was published under this title in 1947.
The translation was made by Abba Eban and is now out of print.
The only other book by Tewfik Al Hakim available in English translation
is his play *The Tree Climber*, translated by Denys Johnson-Davies and published
in 1966 by Oxford University Press, London.

While living through disturbed times, Tewfik Al Hakim's own
life has been comparatively free of dramatic incident; he himself
is of a retiring and reticent nature and though his face is
as familiar in the Arab countries as, say, Bernard Shaw's was in
the English-speaking world, few people know anything of his
private life – that, for instance, despite the playful misogynism
expressed in many of his plays (as for instance in *Fate of a
Cockroach*) he married in 1946 and has a son and a daughter.
Tewfik Al Hakim has never been interested in political creeds
and 'isms'. No Egyptian, however, particularly a writer, can
stand wholly aloof from politics and it is amusing to note that
Tewfik Al Hakim recounts in his autobiography how his first
full-length play, written in 1919 and since lost, dealt with the
British occupation of his country and was entitled *The Unwanted
Guest*. It remained unpublished and unproduced. Over the years
Tewfik Al Hakim has shown great skill – not shared by many of
his fellow authors – in keeping out of political trouble. The
inevitable accusation of living in an ivory tower (he published a
volume of essays under the title *From the Ivory Tower*) has been
levelled against him; while he has never entered any political
arena, he has none the less throughout his career shown himself
deeply concerned with such fundamental and potentially dangerous
issues as justice and truth, good and evil and, above all, freedom.

All four plays in the present volume deal, directly or indirectly,
with some aspect of freedom. In *The Sultan's Dilemma*, which takes
place in the 'Thousand and One Nights' atmosphere of the rule
of a Mameluke sultan, freedom and the choice faced by every
absolute ruler are the themes. Those themes, incidentally, were
as valid for the Egyptian reader in 1960, the year when the play
was published, as for his forbears during the times of the
Mamelukes. In *Fate of a Cockroach*, man's natural love of freedom,
his refusal to despair in the face of adversity, are exemplified in
the cockroach's strivings to climb out of the bath. *The Song of Death*,
the earliest of the four plays and the most local, has as its central
theme the conflict between traditional vengeance – as much a
part of life in rural Egypt as in Sicily – and freedom through
education from such deadening and destructive prejudice. *Not a
Thing out of Place* seems to suggest that while the ultimate in
freedom, anarchy, can be fun, true freedom consists in pursuing
a middle way. Tewfik Al Hakim's preoccupation with freedom
can also be seen from the title of one of his volumes of
autobiography, *The Prison of Life*, in which he discusses the

individual's inability to escape from the imprisonment imposed
upon him by the circumstances of his birth, by the fact that he is
the child of two particular parents with particular attributes who
in turn were brought into the world with inherited characteristics.
Tewfik Al Hakim is the undisputed pioneer of dramatic writing
in Arabic. While Egypt has a theatrical tradition going back more
than a hundred years, the plays produced were until recently
either heavy melodrama adapted into cliché-ridden classical
Arabic from the French or domestic farces, often with political
overtones, written in the colloquial language. With his natural
talent, his wide reading in French, his close study of the
techniques of the European theatre (the dramatic form was
unknown in classical Arabic literature), his interest in the
problems of language – most pertinent in a culture where the
written language differs so much from the spoken – with these
attributes Tewfik Al Hakim gave to the Egyptian theatre the
foundations of respectability it needed. That the theatre in Egypt
today is both a serious and popular form of entertainment and
that it is attracting some of the best talents among the younger
writers is due in large part to the writer of the plays in this
present volume.

DENYS JOHNSON-DAVIES

Fate of a Cockroach

Characters

Cockroaches
KING
QUEEN
MINISTER
SAVANT
PRIEST
A SUBJECT COCKROACH

Procession of Ants

Mortals
SAMIA, a housewife
ADIL, her husband
COOK
DOCTOR

Act One — The Cockroach as King

The scene is a spacious courtyard – as viewed of course by the cockroaches. In actual fact the courtyard is nothing more than the bathroom floor in an ordinary flat. In the front part of this courtyard stands an immense wall, which is nothing but the outer wall of the bath. The time is night, though from the point of view of the cockroaches it is daytime – our bright daylight being so blinding to them that it causes them either to disappear or go to sleep. At the beginning of the play, night has not completely fallen, which is to say that the cockroaches' day is about to begin. The King is standing in sprightly fashion next to a hole in the wall, perhaps the doorway to his palace, and is calling to the Queen who is asleep inside the palace.

KING: Come along – wake up! It's time for work.

QUEEN (*from inside*): The darkness of evening has not yet appeared.

KING: Any moment now it will.

QUEEN: Has the blinding light of day completely disappeared?

KING: Any moment now it will.

QUEEN: Until it disappears completely and night has completely come, let me be and don't bother me.

KING: What laziness! What laziness!

QUEEN (*making her appearance*): I wasn't sleeping. You must remember that I have my toilet and make-up to do.

KING: Make-up and toilet! If all wives were like you, then God help all husbands!

QUEEN (*aroused to anger*): I'm a queen! Don't forget I'm the Queen!

KING: And I'm the King!

QUEEN: I'm exactly the same as you – there's no difference between us at all.

KING: There is a difference.

QUEEN: And what, prithee, might this difference be?

KING: My whiskers.

QUEEN: Just as you have whiskers, so have I.

KING: Yes, but my whiskers are longer than yours.

QUEEN: That is a trifling difference.

KING: So it seems to you.

QUEEN: To you rather. It is your sickly imagination that always makes it appear to you that there is a difference between us.

KING: The difference exists – it can be clearly seen by anyone with eyes to see. If you don't believe me, ask the Minister, the Priest, the Savant, and all those worthy gentlemen connected with the court . . .

QUEEN (*sarcastically*): The court!

KING: Please – no sarcasm! I have an ever-growing feeling that you're always trying to belittle my true worth.

QUEEN: Your worth?

KING: Yes, and my authority. You are always trying to diminish my authority.

QUEEN (*even more sarcastically*): Your authority? Your authority over whom? Not over me at any rate – you are in no way better than me. You don't provide me with food or drink. Have you ever fed me? I feed myself, just as you feed yourself. Do you deny it?

KING: In the whole cockroach kingdom there is no one who feeds another. Every cockroach strives for his own daily bread.

QUEEN: Then I am free to do as I like?

KING: And who ever said you weren't?

QUEEN: Let me be then. It is I who will decide when I shall work and when be lazy, when to sleep and when to get up.

KING: Of course you are free to do as you like but, in your capacity as Queen, you must set a good example.

QUEEN: A good example to whom?

KING: To the subjects, naturally.

QUEEN: The subjects? And where might they be? In my whole life I've never seen anyone around you but those three: the Minister, the Priest, and the learned Savant.

KING: They are enough, they are the élite, the cream . . .

QUEEN: But if you are the King you should be surrounded by the people.

KING: Have you forgotten the characteristics of our species? We are not like those small creatures called 'ants', who gather together in their thousands on the slightest pretext.

QUEEN: Don't remind me of ants! A king like you claiming you have worth and authority and you don't know how to solve the ant problem!

KING: The ant problem! Ah . . . um . . .

QUEEN: Ah . . . um . . . is that all you can say?

KING: What reminded you of ants?

QUEEN: Their being a continual threat to us. A queen like me, in my position and with my beauty, elegance, and pomp, can't take a step without trembling for fear that I might slip and fall on my back – and woe to me should I fall on my back, for I would quickly become a prey to the armies of ants.

KING: Be careful, therefore, that you do not fall on your back!

QUEEN: Is that the only solution you have?

KING: Do you want, from one day to the next, a solution to a problem that is as old as time?

QUEEN: Then shut up and don't boast about the length of your whiskers!

KING: Please! Don't talk to the King in such a tone!

QUEEN: King! I would just like to ask *who* made you a king.

KING: I made myself a king.

QUEEN: And what devious means and measures brought you to the throne and placed you on the seat of kingship?

KING (*indignantly*): Means and measures? Pardon me for saying so, but you're stupid!

QUEEN: I confess I'm stupid about this . . .

KING: What means and what measures, Madam? The question's a lot simpler than that. One morning I woke up and looked at my face in the mirror – or rather in a pool of water near the drain. You yourself know this drain well – it's the one at which we first met. Do you remember?

QUEEN: Of course I remember, but what's the connection between the drain, your face, and the throne?

KING: Have a little patience and you'll find out. I told you that I looked at my face in the mirror – something that you naturally do every day, perhaps every hour, in order to assure yourself of the beauty of your face.

QUEEN: At present we're talking about *your* face. Speak and don't get away from the subject.

KING (*rather put out by now*): As I told you, I looked at my face in the mirror – this was of course by chance . . . that is to say by sheer accident . . . meaning that it was not intentional, I swear to you.

QUEEN: That's neither here nor there. You looked at your face in the drain – what did you discover?

KING: I discovered something that surprised me and aroused in me . . .

QUEEN: A feeling of dejection.

KING: Not at all – of admiration.

QUEEN: Admiration of what?

KING: Of the length of my whiskers. I was really delighted at the length of my whiskers. I immediately rose up and challenged all the cockroaches to compare their whiskers with mine, and that if it was apparent that mine were the longest then I should become king over them all.

QUEEN: And they accepted the challenge?

KING: No, they conceded it to me there and then, saying that they had no time for whisker-measuring.

QUEEN: And so you automatically became His Majesty!

KING: Just so.

QUEEN: And did they tell you what your privileges were to be?

KING: No.

QUEEN: And did they tell you what their duties towards you were?

KING: No. They merely said that as I was pleased with the title and rank, I could do as I pleased. So long as this cost them nothing and they were not required to feed me, then they had no objection to my calling myself what I liked. And so they left me, each going his own way in search of his daily bread.

QUEEN: Then how was it that I became Queen?

KING: By commonsense logic. As I was King and you were the female I loved and lived with, so you were of necessity Queen.

QUEEN: And your Minister? How did he become a minister?

KING: His talents nominated him for the office of Minister, just as mine did for the throne.

QUEEN: We know about your talents – the length of your whiskers. But what are your Minister's talents?

KING: His consummate concern with proposing disconcerting problems and producing unpleasant news.

QUEEN: And the Priest, what are his talents?

KING: The completely incomprehensible things he says.

QUEEN: And the learned Savant?

KING: The strange information he has about things that have no existence other than in his own head.

QUEEN: And what induced you to put up with these people?

KING: Necessity. I found no one but them wanting to be close to

me. They are in need of someone to whom they can pour
out their absurdities, whereas I am in need of close
companions who will call me 'Your Majesty'.

QUEEN: All of which was brought upon you by your long
whiskers.

KING: And am I responsible? I was born with them like this.

QUEEN: Maybe there was someone with longer whiskers than you
and yet he never thought of declaring himself a king.

KING: Very likely, yet it was I who thought . . .

QUEEN: A stupid idea in any case.

KING (*indignantly*): And who are you to say? You understand
nothing!

QUEEN: I understand more than you.

KING: You're a garrulous and conceited cockroach!

QUEEN: And you're a . . .

KING: Hush! The Minister's coming.

QUEEN: Then have some self-respect in front of him and treat me
with respect.

KING: To hear is to obey, Your Majesty.

QUEEN: That's better! Husbands like you are submissive only to
a woman who maintains her rights.

The Minister makes his appearance, wailing.

MINISTER: My Lord King! Help, my Lord King!

KING: What is it?

MINISTER: A calamity! A great calamity, my Lord!

KING: Goodness gracious! (*aside*) I told you his hobby was to
bring unpleasant news. (*loudly*) Yes? Tell us, delight our ears!

MINISTER: My son, Your Majesty – my one and only son.

KING: What's wrong with him?

MINISTER: He has been taken in the prime of youth – has died
in the spring of life – he has been killed! Killed!

KING: Killed? How? Who killed him?

MINISTER: The ants.

KING: The ants again?

QUEEN: There, you see? The ants. The ants.

MINISTER: Yes, Your Majesty, the ants – none but the ants.

KING: Ah, those ants! Tell us what happened.

MINISTER: What always happens.

KING: Be more explicit.

MINISTER: My son was walking along the wall, just going for a stroll for amusement's sake, like anyone else at his age – a perfectly innocent stroll of course, for you well know what a well-behaved person he is. He's exceedingly serious, with no inclinations towards flirtations or foolhardy ventures, all those kinds of nonsensical pastimes ...

KING (*impatiently*): That's neither here nor there – what happened?

MINISTER: His foot slipped and he fell to the ground. Of course he fell on his back and was unable to turn on to his front and get to his feet. And then the ants spotted him. They brought along their troops and armies, surrounded him, smothered him, and carried him off to their towns and villages.

QUEEN: What a terrible thing! Truly a catastrophe!

MINISTER: A great catastrophe, Your Majesty – a national catastrophe!

KING: I share your feelings of sadness for the deceased. Don't, though, ask that I announce public mourning.

MINISTER: I have not asked for an announcement of mourning, Your Majesty.

KING: That's extremely intelligent of you.

MINISTER: I am merely announcing that it is a catastrophe for the whole of our species.

KING: The whole of our species? The death of your son?

MINISTER: I mean rather the ants' aggression against us all in this manner.

QUEEN (*to the Minister*): He understands what you mean perfectly well. He merely pretends not to. He turns the matter into a personal one so that he need not bother himself about the decisive solution which everyone awaits from him.

KING: What are you saying? Are you trying to accuse me of neglecting the duties of my position?

QUEEN: I am not accusing you, I am merely drawing your attention to the necessity for finding a solution to the problem of the ants.

KING: And is the problem of the ants a new one? Speak, Minister?

MINISTER: No, Your Majesty.

KING: Then you know that it is not new, that it is old as Time itself.

MINISTER: Certainly, Your Majesty.

KING: We grew up, our fathers, our grandfathers, and our grandfathers' grandfathers grew up, with the problem of the ants there.

MINISTER: Truly, Your Majesty.

KING: Seeing that you know all that, why do you today assign me the task of solving it? Why should it be my bad luck that I, out of all those fathers and grandfathers who came before me, should alone be asked to find the solution?

QUEEN: Because before you came along there had been no one who was so delighted with the length of his whiskers that he demanded to be made king!

KING: Shut up, you . . .

QUEEN: Mind what you say!

KING (*between his teeth*): Your . . . Your Majesty!

QUEEN: Yes, that's the polite way in which you should address me.

KING: And with all politeness I would like to ask you how you know that before me there was no cockroach who wanted to be king?

QUEEN: Because such ideas only occur to someone like you.

KING: Like me?

QUEEN: Yes, because you're my husband and I know you well.

KING: Kindly note that we are not alone now, also that I am now fulfilling my official functions.

QUEEN: Go ahead and fulfil your official functions!

KING: Speak, Minister.

MINISTER: Before you, Your Majesty, we lived in an age of primitive barbarism. We had neither a king nor a minister, then you came along, with your sense of organization and sound thinking, and ascended the throne.

KING: Then I have a sense of organization and sound thinking?

MINISTER: Without doubt, Your Majesty.

KING: Tell Her Majesty that!

QUEEN (*sarcastically*): Her Majesty is primarily concerned with the practical results. I want to see the fruit of this thinking and organization. Come on, produce a solution to the problem of the ants!

KING (*impatiently*): Come along, Minister – suggest something!

MINISTER: As you think best, Your Majesty.

KING: Yes, but it's up to you first to put forward an opinion, even if it's a stupid one. I'll then look into it.

MINISTER: Put forward an opinion?

KING: Yes, any opinion. Speak – quickly. It's one of the duties of your position to put forward an opinion – and for me to make fun of it.

QUEEN: Perhaps his opinion will be sound.

KING: I don't think so – I know his opinions.

QUEEN: Why, then, did you appoint him Minister?

KING: I didn't appoint him. I told you so a thousand times – I never appointed anyone. It's he who appointed himself. I accepted because he had no rival.

MINISTER: I volunteered to act without a salary.

KING: Talk seriously, Minister, and don't waste the State's time.

MINISTER: I've found it! Your Majesty, I think we could overcome the ants with the same weapon they use.

KING: And what's their weapon?

MINISTER: Armies. They attack us with huge armies. Now if we were able to mobilize ourselves and assemble in great numbers we'd find it easy to attack them, to scatter and to crush them under our great feet.

KING: A stupid idea.

QUEEN: Why do you make fun of it before you have discussed it?

KING: It's clearly unacceptable and absurd.

QUEEN: First of all, encourage him to speak and then talk things over with him.

KING (turning to Minister; peevishly): I have encouraged you and here I am talking things over with you. Speak. Tell me how many there will be in the army of cockroaches you want to mobilize?

MINISTER: Let's say twenty. Twenty cockroaches assembled together could trample underfoot and destroy a long column of ants – nay, a whole village, a whole township.

KING: Of that there is no doubt, but has it ever happened in the whole of our long history that twenty cockroaches have gathered together in one column?

MINISTER: It has not, but we can try . . .

KING: How can we try? We are quite different from ants. The ants know the discipline of forming themselves into columns, but we cockroaches don't know discipline.

MINISTER: Perhaps by learning and training . . .

KING: And who will teach and train us.

MINISTER: We can look around for someone who will undertake it.

KING: Marvellous! So we end up with looking around for a teacher and a trainer! Tell me, then, if we find the teacher and the trainer, after how many generations will the species of cockroaches be taught and trained to walk in columns?

MINISTER: Such information, Your Majesty, does not fall within my province. I have merely given my opinion as to the plan of action. It is for others to talk about the details.

KING: Who are those others? For example?

MINISTER: Our learned Savant for example. He is the man to be asked about such information.

QUEEN: He is right. These are things about which the learned Savant can talk.

KING: And where is the learned Savant?

MINISTER: We'll ask him to come immediately, Your Majesty.

KING: Ask for him and let him come – we are waiting.

Hardly has the Minister made a move than the learned Savant makes his appearance, panting.

MINISTER *(to the Savant)*: My dear chap, we were just about to inquire about you. His Majesty wants you on an important matter.

SAVANT: Good.

MINISTER: His Majesty will tell you . . .

KING: No, you tell him.

MINISTER: Shall I put the whole matter to him?

KING: Yes – quickly.

MINISTER: The matter in question is the problem of the ants.

SAVANT: What about the problem of the ants?

MINISTER: We want to find a decisive solution to it.

SAVANT: And what have I to do with this? This is a political problem. It is for you to solve – you in your capacity as Minister and His Majesty in his capacity as King.

MINISTER *(now baffled)*: A political problem?

SAVANT: In any case, it's an old problem. It does not fall within the province of science or scientists.

KING: But the Minister has turned it into a scientific problem, because he wants the cockroaches to be taught to walk in columns.

SAVANT: That can never happen.

MINISTER: But it must do, because we can't go on like this for ever, having the ants attacking us and not being able to drive them off.

QUEEN: The Minister is right, we must think seriously about this danger.

SAVANT: What exactly is required of me?

QUEEN: To assist with your knowledge. All hope now lies with science.

SAVANT: Define exactly what is required. What is required of me precisely? In science things must be precisely defined.

QUEEN: Define things for him, Minister.

MINISTER: You know that the ants attack us with their armies. If we also were able to mobilize an army of twenty, or even ten, cockroaches with which to attack them, we would be able to destroy their towns and villages.

SAVANT: Then mobilize ten cockroaches!

MINISTER: And who will do so?

SAVANT: You and His Majesty the King – that's your job.

KING: Our job!

SAVANT: Naturally. If the King can't order ten cockroaches to assemble together, then what authority has the King got?

KING (*haughtily*): It seems that you're living in a daze, learned Savant!

MINISTER: The problem is how to gather these cockroaches together.

KING: Tell him! Tell him!

QUEEN: Inform us, Savant, has it ever hapened that you have seen ten cockroaches gathered together in one spot?

SAVANT: Yes, I once saw – a very long time ago, in the early days of my youth – several cockroaches gathered together at night in the kitchen round a piece of tomato.

QUEEN: Tomato?

SAVANT: Yes.

KING: An extraordinary idea – this matter of a tomato!

MINISTER: We begin from here.

QUEEN: And you say that science cannot solve the problem?

SAVANT: What has science to do with this? That was no more than a general observation.

KING: This is the modesty of a true Savant. The idea is, however, useful. If we were able to get a piece of tomato, then a number of cockroaches would gather together round it.

SAVANT: The real problem is how to get hold of a piece of tomato.

KING: How is it, therefore, that we do sometimes get hold of a piece?

SAVANT: By sheer chance.

QUEEN: And when does sheer chance occur?

SAVANT: That is something one cannot predict.

KING: You have therefore arrived at solving one problem by presenting us with another.

QUEEN: Suggest for us something other than tomatoes.

SAVANT: Any other sort of food puts us in the same position, for though we can find food we are unable to make a particular sort of food available.

QUEEN: Can't we get cockroaches together without food?

SAVANT: Neither cockroaches nor anything else.

MINISTER: That's true. The armies of the ant species themselves assemble only round food, to carry off food, or to store food.

KING: Our sole method of getting cockroaches together is food?

SAVANT: That's right – from the theoretical point of view.

QUEEN: What do you mean?

SAVANT: I mean, Your Majesty, from the practical point of view it's all neither here nor there, because the cockroaches assembling round the food won't make a bit of difference – they'll just eat and fill their stomachs, then each will take himself off.

KING: That's true. It has happened before. Remember how after I was installed as King a number of cockroaches happened to assemble round a piece of sugar we found – it was sheer good luck – and I seized the opportunity of this gathering to deliver the speech from the throne. I rose to my feet to speak, with them having eaten their fill, and hardly had I uttered two words than I found each one of them waving his whiskers and going off on his own. They left me shouting into thin air!

MINISTER: That's just our trouble!

QUEEN: Is there no cure for this, O Savant?

SAVANT: It is something ingrained.

QUEEN: There must be a reason.

SAVANT: I have thought about this a lot and have hit upon a reason. The fact is that a strong link has been observed between the assembling of cockroaches in one place and the occurrence of catastrophes of a certain sort.

MINISTER: You mean the moving mountains?

SAVANT: Exactly – and the annihilating, choking rain.

KING: That's true. I have heard news of just such calamities.

SAVANT: This has today become confirmed from a scientific point of view. If a number of cockroaches gather together in one place, and there is bright, dazzling light, mountains that have neither pinnacles nor peaks move and trample upon our

troop, utterly squashing them. At other times there teems
down a choking rain that destroys every one of us.

QUEEN: And what is the reason for this, O Savant?

SAVANT: Natural phenomena.

KING: And why do these natural phenomena only occur when
several cockroaches are assembled?

SAVANT: Science has not yet arrived at an explanation.

KING: And what is the true nature of these moving mountains
and this annihilating, choking rain?

QUEEN: These moving mountains and this choking rain, are they
intended to destroy us?

SAVANT: These are all questions which cannot be answered
scientifically.

QUEEN: Then why do these catastrophes only occur when we are
assembled together?

SAVANT: I do not know, Your Majesty. All that science can do
is to record these phenomena, to link up the connection
between them and deduce a scientific law.

KING: You mean to say therefore that our fear of such calamities
has made our species from time immemorial afraid of
assembling together?

SAVANT: Exactly, it is from here that this characteristic has
arisen – the fact that each one of us goes off on his own in a
different direction: an instinctive defence mechanism.

MINISTER: But the ants do exactly the opposite to us.

SAVANT: The ants, because of their tiny size, can do what they
like, but we larger creatures are in a special position.

MINISTER: But by their coming together they overcome us.

SAVANT: Yes – regretfully.

MINISTER: And the solution? We want a solution, O Savant.

KING: The Minister's son was torn to pieces by troops of ants
who carried him off to their villages.

SAVANT: My sincere condolences, Minister.

MINISTER: Thank you, but this is not all we expect of you.

KING: That's right – we want of you something more useful than
merely condoling with the Minister.

QUEEN: We want a definite remedy.

SAVANT: Give me time in which to examine the matter. With me
everything must be done on a proper basis, with one step
following another. First we must start by knowing ourselves,
by discovering what is round about us in this vast cosmos. Do
you know for example what is to be found behind this shiny

wall underneath which we stand? (*He points at the outer wall of the bath.*)

KING: What is there behind it?

SAVANT: I have climbed to the top of it many times and have seen the strangest of things.

ALL: What did you see?

SAVANT: I saw a vast chasm – probably a large lake, though the strange thing is that it is sometimes without water, at others full of water.

ALL: And why is that?

SAVANT: I do not yet know, but after having observed this phenomenon, I was able to observe a constant factor, namely that this lake was full of water in the glare of light, but was empty of water in the darkness.

KING: And what is the relationship between light and the water?

SAVANT: There is some sort of relationship but I do not yet know the reason for it. Nevertheless we have been able to deduce a constant law in the form of a true scientific equation, namely that light equals water and darkness equals dryness.

KING: At such a moment, therefore . . .

SAVANT: At such a moment the lake is dry and it has a very beautiful appearance. Its sides are smooth and snow-white – as though strewn with jasmine flowers.

QUEEN: I wish I could see them.

SAVANT: With great pleasure. If Your Majesty would permit me, I shall lead you to the top of the wall, and then you can look down at the deep chasm – a marvellous sight.

KING: I too would like to see it.

SAVANT: I am at your disposal – let's all go.

MINISTER: Wait – the Priest is coming.

The Priest makes his appearance.

KING: Come and join us, O venerable Priest!

PRIEST: That's exactly what I'd like to do, for I have just passed by a most sad sight.

KING: A sad sight?

PRIEST: Yes, a procession of ants carrying a cockroach. The cockroach, it seems, was dead and motionless. An ant at the head was dragging him by his whiskers, while at the rear a group of them were pushing him. There was nothing I could do but to ask the gods to have mercy on him.

QUEEN: Do you not know who it was?

PRIEST: No.

QUEEN: That was the Minister's son.

PRIEST (*turning to the Minister*): Your son?

MINISTER (*lowering his head in sorrow*): Yes.

PRIEST: May the gods grant you comfort! I shall say a prayer for you.

MINISTER: Thank you!

KING: We were just now discussing what we should do about these catastrophes, for the time has come to search for a remedy. Have you any suggestion, O Priest?

PRIEST: I have only one suggestion.

KING: Don't you dare say to offer up sacrifices!

PRIEST: There is nothing else.

MINISTER: Do you see, Majesty? We have now entered into another difficulty – the search for sacrifices. We may find them and we may not. Also, who will go looking for them and bring them back? I personally am not prepared to do so – my psychological state does not permit me.

SAVANT: I certainly am not prepared to do so, because I naturally do not believe in such methods.

PRIEST: Apostasy is rife in this kingdom!

QUEEN: Do not say such a thing, O Priest! You know well that I am a firm believer.

KING: Yes, we are believers, but the question of these sacrifices has become tiresome – and a trifle old-fashioned. In the past we have offered some of the sacrifices you demanded but they gave no result.

PRIEST: The result is not in my hands – I offer the sacrifices and the gods are free to accept or refuse them.

SAVANT: Your gods always refuse the sacrifices – only the ants accept them.

MINISTER: Truly. We noticed that with the piece of sugar you demanded as a sacrifice – it was the ants who ate it.

KING: Listen, O Priest – ask the gods to help us without it costing us anything.

PRIEST: Do you want them to serve you for free?

MINISTER: And why not? Does not our King undertake his official duties for free?

QUEEN: And I myself – the Queen – no one has given me anything, not even my dear husband. I strive for my daily bread like him, without any difference at all.

SAVANT: Nor I of course – no one has laid down any salary or wage for me.

MINISTER: Nor I too. I am the Minister of the kingdom and all my official functions are performed for no wage.

KING: Then why do you demand wages for your gods?

PRIEST: I will not *demand* anything.

KING: On the contrary, you must demand of them that they help us, but on the condition that such help is free and for nothing – god-sent!

PRIEST: I can't put conditions on the gods.

SAVANT: Do they stipulate the fee to you, or do you volunteer it?

PRIEST: There is no stipulation or volunteering, but anyone who asks something of someone should aim to tempt him.

SAVANT: So it's a question of tempting . . .

PRIEST: Describe it how you will, but I cannot make a request of the gods while I am empty-handed.

SAVANT: And do you think the gods are concerned with what you have in your hands?

PRIEST: What kind of question is that?

SAVANT: Have the gods ever listened to you?

PRIEST: Naturally.

SAVANT: When was that?

PRIEST: Once, I was lying ill in a corner when I saw the armies of ants approaching. I was certain that I was done for. I called upon the gods with a prayer that came from the depths of my heart. Suddenly I saw that something looking like a large dark cloud full of water had descended from the skies and swooped down upon the armies of ants and swept them quite away, clearing them off the face of the earth.

QUEEN: How extraordinary!

SAVANT: The scientific composition of this cloud is well known: it consists of a network of many threads from a large piece of moistened sacking.

KING: Neither the cloud's origin nor yet its scientific composition is of interest. What is important is who sent it down and wiped away the ants with it.

PRIEST: Speak to him, O King, and ask him who sent it down from the sky and with it destroyed the armies of the ants. Who? Who?

SAVANT: This is not a question that science can answer.

However, I very much doubt the existence of any connection between this priest's prayer and the descent of this cloud.

PRIEST: How is it then that the cloud descended only after my prayer?

SAVANT: Pure coincidence.

PRIEST: What blasphemy! What apostasy!

QUEEN: I am against blasphemy and apostasy, and you, my husband who are King, must be like me in this.

KING: Of course I am like you in this. Listen, O reverend Priest, I believe, must believe, that your prayer was beneficial. In any event, seeing that your prayer was efficacious and successful the once, it will clearly be so again. I would therefore ask you to pray and pray long.

MINISTER: Particularly as cost-free prayer without sacrifice has been successful.

QUEEN: Because, as he said, it issued forth from the depths of his heart.

PRIEST (*irritably*): Yes, all right – I shall pray.

QUEEN (*shouting*): Look! Look!

A procession of ants carrying a cockroach makes its appearance.

THE ANTS (*chanting*):

> *Here is your great feast.*
> *We carry it together, together,*
> *To our towns, our villages:*
> *A great and splendid cockroach –*
> *Provision for the winter long.*
> *With it our storerooms we shall fill.*
> *None of us will hunger know,*
> *Because we all lend a hand,*
> *We're members of a single body.*
> *There is amongst us no one sad,*
> *There is amongst us none who's lonesome,*
> *There is amongst us none who says*
> *'I am not concerned with others.'*

The ants move towards the wall with their heavy load, while the cockroaches continue to watch them in glum silence and stupefaction.

KING: It grieves us, O Minister, to see your son borne off in this manner.

PRIEST: May the gods have mercy upon him! May the gods have
mercy upon him!

KING: It's certainly a most dignified funeral!

SAVANT: So it seems, although logic dictates that it should be
otherwise, for in relation to the ants it means food, that is to
say a universal blessing, and the carrying of blessings and
food should be accompanied by manifestations of joy,
acclamations and singing.

KING: But we hear nothing – groups walking in utter silence.

SAVANT: That is so. We hear no sound from them because they
are such tiny creatures. Who knows, though – perhaps they are
making thunderous sounds?

KING: Perhaps they have a language?

SAVANT: Perhaps they were singing?

KING: Naturally – for them – this was a most suitable occasion
for joy and singing.

QUEEN: I implore you! I implore you! Do not stir up the grief of
a sorrowing father with such talk! Let us either do something
for him or keep quiet.

KING: Forgive me, Minister, this was merely general talk about
the ants, but – as the Queen says – something must be done,
and this has occupied us since our meeting up today.

QUEEN: This meeting which up till now has achieved nothing
useful.

KING: My dear! My dear! Your Majesty! We are still at the
stage of conferring and exchanging points of view.

QUEEN: What conferring and what points of view? There are the
ants in front of you! They are carrying off the Minister's son
to make a good, wholesome meal of him. Is it so difficult for
you, being as you are four hulking males, to attack and crush
them, and to rescue the Minister's son from their hands?

KING: Are we four? Where's the fourth?

QUEEN: You of course.

KING: Ah, quite right. But I . . . leave me out of it. I am the
King and the King rules and does not fight.

PRIEST: Leave me also out of it. I am the Priest and the Priest
prays and does not fight.

SAVANT: And I too, naturally. You must leave me out of it, for
I am the Savant and the Savant makes research but does not
brawl.

QUEEN: Then I shall go – I, the Queen – yet I shall not say I

am the Queen, but merely a female. Stand, you males, and
watch with folded arms while females go to war.

KING: And the Minister? Is he not a male like us? Why is he
standing by silently when the matter concerns him?

MINISTER: I do not want to put you in such predicaments
because of my son.

QUEEN: As we have said, the matter is no longer merely that of
your son.

MINISTER: I am grateful, Your Majesty, but . . .

QUEEN: The question is too important to be purely a personal
one – they all know that, these most excellent leaders of the
Kingdom. However, they don't want to know so they
pretend not to, because they are without resolution, without
willpower.

KING: My dear Majesty . . .

QUEEN: Shut up, you effete weakling! Leave the matter in my
hands!

KING: Do you want me to give up the throne in your favour?

QUEEN: No, my dear sir. This throne of yours does not interest
me, does not tempt me. All I want is for you to let me act.

KING: Don't be so headstrong, my dear. You can do nothing.
You want to attack, to make war, and to fight like the ants,
but this cannot happen.

QUEEN: And why not?

KING: Ask the eminent Savant – he has the answer.

QUEEN: Speak, O eminent Savant!

KING: Speak and tell her why the ants know methods of warfare
and we don't. Tell her, explain to her!

SAVANT: First, the ants have a Minister of War.

QUEEN: A Minister of War?

SAVANT: Naturally. A minister who devotes all his attention to
the business of organizing armies. Is it reasonable that all
these vast troops should march with such discipline and order
in serried ranks without somebody responsible behind them,
somebody specialized in organizing them?

QUEEN: The question's a simple one – why don't we too have a
specialized Minister of War?

SAVANT: That is a political matter, and I don't understand
politics. Ask His Majesty about that.

QUEEN: Please be so good as to reply, Your Majesty!

KING: What's the question?

QUEEN: Why do you not appoint a specialized Minister of War?

KING: A specialized Minister of War? Is that in my hands? Where is he? Let me find him and I'll appoint him immediately. We had quite enough trouble finding one Minister, our friend here. He was good enough to accept being a general minister to look after everything without understanding anything.

MINISTER: If I do not enjoy your confidence, then I am ready to proffer my resignation.

KING: Your resignation? Do you hear? Now here's our one and only minister threatening to resign!

QUEEN: No, honourable Minister. You enjoy the confidence of everyone. Don't listen to what the King says – he sometimes lets his tongue run away with him.

MINISTER: My thanks to Your Majesty!

KING: Your most gracious Majesty!

QUEEN: Then, O venerable Savant, the whole difference is that the ants have a specialized Minister of War?

SAVANT: That is not all they have.

QUEEN: What do they have as well?

SAVANT: A brilliant Minister of Supply.

QUEEN: A Minister of Supply?

SAVANT: A brilliant one – the operation of storing food in warehouses on that enormous scale must have some remarkable economic planning behind it.

KING: We have no need for any supply or any Minister of Supply, because we don't have a food crisis and have no need to plan or store.

SAVANT: Certainly, our economy runs by sheer good luck – and we boast about it!

QUEEN: Boast about it?

KING: Certainly, my dear. Certainly we have many things to boast about which should not be sneezed at.

SAVANT: In confirmation of His Majesty's opinion I would say that we have a characteristic not found among the ants, namely birth control. The ants let their numbers increase so enormously that they are driven into a food and storage crisis, and the need for food leads to war.

KING: We are certainly in no need of food, of the storage of food, or of war.

SAVANT: And so we are superior creatures.

KING: Without doubt. We attack no living creature; we harm no one. We do not know greed or the desire to acquire and store things away.

QUEEN: Are there no creatures superior to us?

SAVANT: No, we are the most superior creatures on the face of the earth.

QUEEN: That's right, and yet we suffer because of those other, inferior creatures.

SAVANT: Inferiority is always a cause of trouble, but we must be patient. We cannot bring those creatures who are lower than us up to the same standard of civilization as ourselves. To each his own nature, his own environment, and his own circumstances. The ant, for instance, is concerned solely with food. As for us, we are more concerned with knowledge.

QUEEN: Knowledge?

SAVANT: Certainly. These long whiskers we have we do not use only to touch food. Very often we touch with them things which are not eaten, merely in order to seek out their nature, to discover their reality. Do you not, Your Majesty, often do just that?

QUEEN: Certainly. Certainly. I am very interested in touching strange substances with my whiskers, not merely from my desire for food but from sheer curiosity.

SAVANT: Yes, from curiosity, a love of knowledge, a desire to know.

KING: And yet you say, my dear Queen, that we are weak-willed. We are the sturdiest of creatures on earth, is that not so, O venerable Savant?

SAVANT: Most certainly, Majesty.

KING: Are the ants stronger than us? Impossible! They do not know us; all they know is how to eat us. But they do not know who we are. Do the ants know us?

SAVANT: Of course not.

KING: Have they got the slightest idea of the true facts about us, about our nature? Do they realize that we are thinking creatures?

SAVANT: The only knowledge they have about us is that we are food for them.

KING: And so, in relation to ourselves, they are inferior creatures.

QUEEN: Which doesn't prevent them eating us. We must find some way of protecting ourselves from being harmed by them.

KING: The only way is for us not to fall on our backs.

QUEEN: This, then, in your view is the whole solution?

KING: In the view of us all.

QUEEN: We have in short ended up where we began, that is to say at nought, nought, nought! Our meeting, our discussions, our investigations have all led us to nought, nought, nought!

SAVANT: In research there is no such thing as nought. Every investigation is useful. When we touch things with our whiskers we derive profit even though we do not exactly understand the true nature of those things. Which reminds me, a few moments ago I was saying that I had just come from making a very important discovery but no one appeared ready to listen.

KING: Ah, yes, it seems to me that I did hear you say so. And what is the discovery? Speak – I am a ready listener.

SAVANT: This lake . . .

KING: What lake? Ah yes, of course – we were talking about a lake and you wanted to take the Queen and me there so that we might see it.

SAVANT: And we were in fact on the point of going except that the Priest came along.

KING: Yes, that is true. Let us go then. Come, let's go now. That is at least more worthwhile than talking about fairy tales and fanciful projects! After you, my dear Majesty!

QUEEN: I shall not go with you. I shall stay here and the Minister will stay with me. He is naturally in no psychological state for sight-seeing.

KING: As you both wish. And you, O illustrious Priest, will you come with us?

PRIEST: Such reconnoitrings have nothing to do with me.

KING: Then let us away, O Savant!

The King and the Savant go off. The Queen, the Minister and the Priest remain.

QUEEN: I am very sad about your loss. However, I am also sad and distressed about the shameful attitude of my husband.

MINISTER: Do not blame your husband, Your Majesty. Your husband, the King, is capable of doing nothing.

QUEEN: He is at least capable of being serious and of making up his mind; of being up to the situation.

MINISTER: The situation is difficult.

QUEEN: Certainly, and it needs a strong character to face up to it, but I am sorry to say that my husband is of a weak character. Have you not remarked this?

MINISTER: We rely on you, Your Majesty.

QUEEN: Were it not that I am at his side, what would he do? Deep down inside he feels this. I am a stronger personality than he, but he's always trying to fool himself, to make himself out as superior.

MINISTER: We all have our particular natures and characteristics. He is nevertheless good-hearted.

QUEEN: I don't deny that. He is a truly good person but . . .

PRIEST: But going around with that atheist of a Savant and listening to his nonsense bodes no good.

MINISTER: He also listens a lot to you, O venerable Priest!

PRIEST: And likewise he listens to you, O high-minded Minister!

MINISTER: He listens to everyone and to everything. It is only fair of us to say that he is a man with an open mind.

QUEEN: You defend him despite everything because without him you'd be without a job.

MINISTER: I, Your Majesty?

QUEEN: Yes, you. You in particular. The Priest has things to occupy him, so does the Savant, but you the Minister would have no work to do without the King.

MINISTER: And you, Your Majesty? You are the Queen and the Queen . . .

QUEEN: Understood – she too hasn't got a job without the King! I know that.

MINISTER: Sorry, I . . .

QUEEN: Don't apologize! My position is like yours. I know that. The difference, however, is that I'm female and he's always wanting to remind me that he's male – and that he's got longer whiskers than me!

A cockroach appears; he is singing.

COCKROACH (*singing*):   *O night, O lovely night*
During which our eyes we close
On things both dear and dread.
O night, O lovely night.
With one eye we go to sleep,
With the other we impatiently await
The breaking of the lucent dawn.
O night, O lovely night.

QUEEN: Who's that singing?

MINISTER (*looking*): He is a subject cockroach.

QUEEN: One of our subjects? Singing while we're thinking, thinking from early morning about his problem! Bring him here.

MINISTER (*calling to him*): Hey you, come here!

COCKROACH (*approaching*): Yes.

MINISTER: Who are you?

COCKROACH: Someone who sings and strives after his daily bread.

MINISTER: You are singing when we are thinking for you?

COCKROACH: And who asked you to think for me? I think for myself.

MINISTER: I'm the Minister.

COCKROACH (*sarcastically*): It's an honour I'm sure.

MINISTER: We are thinking about an important problem that threatens your life – the problem of the ants. You've come along at the right time. We'd like you and others to co-operate with us. What do you think?

COCKROACH: I think you should let me be.

He turns his back on him and departs singing:

> O night, O lovely night
> During which our eyes we close.

MINISTER (*to the Queen*): It's no good!

QUEEN: It really isn't!

The Savant looks down from on top of the outer wall of the bath.

SAVANT (*calling out from on top of the wall*): Help! Help!

QUEEN: What's happened?

SAVANT: The King.

QUEEN (*anxiously*): What's happened to the King?

SAVANT: His foot slipped – he fell into the lake!

QUEEN: Fallen into the lake? How terrible!

MINISTER: Is the King dead?

SAVANT: Not yet. The lake's dry, it's got no water in it. Its walls are slippery and he's at the foot of them trying to get out.

QUEEN: Then let's go and help him to get out. Help him! Save him! For Heaven's sake, save my husband!

SAVANT (*shouting*): Stay where you are! There is no way of saving him – you can't get down to him.

QUEEN: We must do something for him. Let's all go.

SAVANT: Do not move! The walls along the edge of the lake are slippery and your feet too may slip and you'll fall in.

QUEEN: My husband must be saved! Save my husband! I beseech you – save him!

MINISTER: Yes, the King must be saved!

SAVANT: No one can do so. He is in the very depths of the chasm. The walls are slippery. One's feet will slip on the smooth walls. Only he can save himself, only by his own efforts – or a miracle from the skies!

PRIEST: A miracle from the skies! Now *you* speak of a miracle from the skies!

MINISTER: This is your chance, O Priest!

QUEEN: Yes, I implore you, O Priest, to do something about my husband. I implore you!

PRIEST: Has not this Savant said that there is no one in the Heavens to hear us?

SAVANT: Don't seize the opportunity to be coy! Anyone who is able to do something now should do so.

QUEEN: Yes. Do something, O Priest – please!

MINISTER: It's your duty, O Priest – save the King!

PRIEST: There is nothing for me to do but pray.

MINISTER: Then we ask you to pray.

PRIEST: All of us must pray. Even this Savant must pray with us, but he will not accept to do so.

QUEEN: He will, he will accept for our sake, for the sake of my husband.

SAVANT: I shall accept to do so so that I may invalidate his argument. If there really is someone up there who hears our voices, understands our language, and pays attention to our entreaties, that's fine. If not, we have lost nothing.

MINISTER: So he has accepted.

PRIEST: A most grudging acceptance.

SAVANT: I told you he'd get coy and start making excuses.

MINISTER: Please, O Priest, be obliging.

QUEEN: Be sure that our hearts are all with you at this moment.

PRIEST: Not all of you.

MINISTER: Pay no heed to him. Pretend he's not here. Won't our three voices suffice?

SAVANT: I said I would join my voice to yours – what more do
  you want of me?

PRIEST: I don't want your voice to be with ours – it's enough to
  have one doubting voice to spoil the rest.

SAVANT: And what's my voice to you? Is it being addressed to
  you or to the Heavens? Leave it to the Heavens to
  listen or not, whether you yourself accept or not.

MINISTER: That is reasonable.

QUEEN: Truly. Leave the matter to the Heavens, oh venerable
  Priest, and don't bother yourself about it. Who knows?
  Maybe, unbeknownst to us, it will be acceptable.

PRIEST: So be it!

QUEEN: Then let us all pray.

PRIEST: Pray! Lift up your hands with me! Oh gods!

ALL (*lifting up their hands and calling out*): Oh gods! Oh gods!

CURTAIN

Act Two — The Cockroach's Struggle

A bedroom with a bed, a wardrobe, and a small table on which rests an alarm clock. A large table stands between two chairs: on it are papers and books. The room has a small door leading to the bathroom, which contains a bath and a basin with a mirror above it, also a shelf on which are toothbrushes and tubes of toothpaste. From the bedroom another door opens onto the rest of the flat. The room is rather dark; day is beginning to dawn, light seeping through the room. As it gets lighter, Adil suddenly sits up and then gets out of bed; he performs various vigorous gymnastic movements. His wife Samia wakes up and half rises in the bed. She puts on a small bedside light.

SAMIA *(turning to her husband)*: You're up, Adil?

ADIL: Of course.

SAMIA: Has the alarm gone off?

ADIL: Of course not – as usual I got up by myself.

SAMIA: What an odd alarm! Didn't we set it for six before going to bed?

ADIL: We did – as we do every night. However, it waits till I get up by myself and then rings. *(The alarm clock goes off.)*

SAMIA: There – it's ringing.

ADIL: It does it on purpose, I assure you.

SAMIA: No harm done so long as you're . . .

ADIL: As I'm ringing in its stead?

SAMIA: And that you wake up on time.

ADIL: For you that's all that matters.

He moves towards the bathroom.

SAMIA: Where are you going?

ADIL: To the bathroom of course.

SAMIA *(jumping out of bed)*: Off with you – I'm first.

ADIL: Yes, as usual. I get up before you and it's you who get to the bathroom before me.

SAMIA: That's only right.

ADIL: How is it right? As I wake up before you I should have
the bathroom first. From today onwards I'm sticking to my
rights.

SAMIA: You say that every day – it's a record I've heard only too
often.

ADIL: Because it's my right! It's my right, I say!

SAMIA: Off with you! Don't waste time! I'm going in before you
because my work demands . . .

ADIL: Your work! I suppose I'm out of work? If you're a
company employee, I happen to be also employed by the
same company, and if you're in a hurry so am I. Besides, I've
got to shave which you haven't.

SAMIA: I've got something more important than having to shave.

ADIL: And what might that be?

SAMIA: To do my make-up, my dear man. You don't have to
make up.

ADIL: And what do you have to make up for when you're going
off to work in an oils, paints, and chemicals factory?

SAMIA: What a fatuous question!

ADIL: Give me an answer.

SAMIA: Listen! Don't waste any more time. Please get away from
the bathroom and let me in.

ADIL: No, you don't! Today I'll not weaken – I'll stick to my
rights. I'll not give in today.

SAMIA: You're rebelling?

ADIL: Yes.

SAMIA: You say 'yes'?

ADIL: Yes.

SAMIA: And you repeat it?

ADIL: Yes.

SAMIA: I warn you. This is a warning.

ADIL: What are you going to do?

SAMIA: Get out of my way – at once!

ADIL: Only over my dead body!

SAMIA: Is that so? All right, then!

She pushes him roughly. He almost falls, but catches hold of the bed.

ADIL: Good God! Have you gone crazy, Samia? Why are you
shoving me about like this?

SAMIA: It's you who wants to use force. Everything can be settled
nice and quietly. 'Bye!

*She enters the bathroom. He hurries after her. She locks the bathroom
door in his face. He raps on it.*

ADIL: Open it! Open it! This is no way to behave! It's not a
question of force. You seize your rights by force – I mean my
rights. It's my right. You seize my right by sheer force. Open
up! Open up!

SAMIA (*inside the bathroom – she is doing her hair in front of the mirror
and humming to herself*): Please shut up. Don't annoy me by
knocking like that!

ADIL: By what right do you go in before me?

SAMIA: I came in and there's an end to it.

ADIL: But it's a matter of principle.

SAMIA: A matter of what?

ADIL: Of principle – of principles. Don't you know what
principles are?

SAMIA: I haven't yet read the morning papers.

ADIL: What *are* you talking about?

SAMIA: I'm telling you to occupy yourself usefully until I've
finished having my bath.

ADIL: Occupy myself?

SAMIA: Yes, with anything, because I want quiet – quiet.

ADIL: Quiet? You tell me to be quiet?

SAMIA: Listen, Adil, turn on the radio.

ADIL: Turn on what?

SAMIA (*turning on the basin tap*): Turn the tap on.

ADIL: The tap? You want me to turn the tap on for you as well?
But the tap's where you are.

SAMIA: I told you to turn on the radio.

ADIL: The radio?

SAMIA: Yes, the radio.

ADIL: You said the tap.

SAMIA: The tap? Would I be so crazy as to say such a thing? I
told you to turn on the radio! The radio! Can you hear me
properly?

ADIL: I'm sorry, it's my fault. It's always my fault.

SAMIA (*moistening the toothbrush and taking up the tube of toothpaste*):
What horrible toothpaste! One of your lordship's purchases!

ADIL (*going towards the radio standing on the table*): Why am I so
weak with you? But – but is it really weakness? No, it's
impossible – it's merely that I spoil you. I spoil you because
you're a woman, a weak woman, the weaker sex.

(*He turns on the radio and the voice of the announcer bursts forth.*)

ANNOUNCER: And here is the summary of the news: The black
    nationals rose up in revolt following the occupation by the
    white colonialists by force of . . .
ADIL (*lowering the volume*): They rose up in revolt!
SAMIA: I told you to turn on the radio.
ADIL: It's on.
SAMIA: But I can't hear any singing or music.
ADIL: It's the news. The news! Am I also responsible for the
    radio programmes?
SAMIA: Turn to another station, man.
ADIL: As you say.

He turns to another station and a song is heard:

> '*The attainment of desires in not by hoping;*
> *Things of this world are gained by striving.*'

SAMIA (*humming the song to herself in the bathroom*): 'Things of
    this world are gained . . .'
ADIL: Happy?
SAMIA: Of course – it's a beautiful song.
ADIL: Things of this world are gained by striving! (*He lowers the
    volume.*)
ADIL (*forcefully*): Look here, Samia! Open up! Open up! I want
    to say something important to you!
SAMIA: I haven't had my bath yet.
ADIL: I want to know, I want a quick explanation: Who am I?
SAMIA: What are you saying?
ADIL: I'm asking you who I am.
SAMIA: What a question! You're Adil of course.
ADIL: Adil who?
SAMIA: Adil my husband.
ADIL: Is that all?
SAMIA: What do you mean? Do you want your surname, job,
    and date of birth? It's all written down for you on your
    identity card.
ADIL: I know. I wasn't asking about that. I was asking about my
    true identity. Do you know what my true identity is?
SAMIA: No, you tell me.
ADIL: I'm the world!

SAMIA: The world?

ADIL: Yes, the world that is gained by striving. You take everything I have and I take nothing of yours. You get hold of the whole of my salary and I can't touch a millieme of yours. All the payments, expenses, bills, instalments, all come out of *my* pocket: *your* dressmaker – *your* hairdresser – the instalments on *your* car – *your* petrol – *your* 'fridge – *your* washing machine – *your* Butagas . . .

SAMIA: My Butagas? Talking about the Butagas, listen, Adil – don't forget to get in touch with them to send a fresh bottle.

ADIL: And it's I who always has to get in touch!

SAMIA: I've got work to do as you know.

ADIL: And I've got no work? Your job's *work* and mine's play?

SAMIA: Won't you stop tyrannizing me with your chatter!

ADIL: And now it's I who tyrannize you!

SAMIA: Please – I've got a headache. I want to have my bath in peace – in peace, do you hear? I've told you a thousand times to occupy yourself with something, man. Read the morning paper, take a needle and thread and sew the buttons on your shirt, get the breakfast ready . . .

ADIL: Shall I get your breakfast?

SAMIA: Yes, instead of talking a lot of rubbish.

ADIL (*sitting on his bed and placing his head in the palms of his hands*): Ah . . .

SAMIA: Why are you so quiet? (*Adil remains gloomily immersed in silence.*) Adil! (*Adil does not reply. He gets up and walks about the room.*) Why are you so quiet, Adil? What are you doing out there? (*Adil does not reply but stands himself in front of her framed photo standing on the table by the bed.*) Why don't you reply, Adil? Are you in the room?

ADIL: Yes, in the room.

SAMIA: What are you doing now?

ADIL: I'm looking at your picture.

He is in fact looking at the picture – but with fury; he makes a gesture of wanting to strangle her.

SAMIA: Are you looking at my picture?

ADIL: Yes – with longing.

SAMIA: Is this the time for it? I told you to do something useful.

ADIL: Such as?

SAMIA: Go to the kitchen and put on the milk to heat until the

cook comes. By the way, did you turn on the Butagas? I'll
be lighting the water heater in a while – are you listening?

ADIL: I'm listening.

SAMIA: Hurry up and do it, please.

ADIL: Certainly. This is unnatural. It must be that I'm not a
normal person. (*He knocks at the bathroom door.*)

SAMIA (*cleaning her teeth and rinsing her mouth*): What do you want?

ADIL (*shouting*): I'm not a normal person! Can you hear? Not
normal!

SAMIA: Not normal? Who's not normal?

ADIL: I'm not – I'm not normal.

SAMIA: Are you ill?

ADIL: I shall carry out your orders: the Butagas – the heater –
the bath – the heater – the bath – the Butagas – the heater –
the bath – the bath – the bath –

SAMIA: Hurry up, Adil!

ADIL: Right away. (*He goes to the telephone on the table, lifts the
receiver and dials a number.*) Hullo. Hullo. Raafat? Good
morning, Raafat. Listen. Listen. No, no, I'm not upset. Do
you think I sound upset? No, no, not at all. I . . . I'm only
. . . tell me: are you awake? Ah, of course you're awake
seeing that you're talking to me. No, no . . . I meant . . .
have you had your bath? Oh yes . . . good. No, I haven't
done anything yet. I got up early. That's the root of the
problem. Tell me, talking about baths . . . yes, baths . . . has
your wife . . . no, sorry . . . it's a stupid question. No, no,
nothing. I only wanted to talk to you, merely to . . . merely
to . . . nothing. Yes. Yes. Nothing at all. No, no . . . don't be
alarmed. I'm only . . . actually, I feel that I'm . . . yes, I'm
not completely all right. No, it's not all that bad. Of course
I'll go out. Yes, we'll meet at the factory as usual. Samia . . .
she's in the bath. In the bath, old man . . . in the bath. I'll
give her your regards. No, no, don't worry yourself. I'm fine
. . . fine, Raafat. 'Bye. 'Bye.

*During the telephone conversation Samia has been trying in vain to
put on the water heater. At last, as Adil puts down the receiver, she
opens the door.*

SAMIA: Your lordship was chatting on the telephone while I
thought you'd gone to the kitchen to put on the Butagas.

ADIL: A hurried conversation.

SAMIA: With someone at the company?

ADIL: With a lady.

SAMIA: A lady?

ADIL: Yes, a lady . . . a friend.

SAMIA: Do I know her?

ADIL: No, she's a new friend – a most pleasant person.

SAMIA: Married?

ADIL: Of course not.

SAMIA: Someone who works in the company?

ADIL: No, someone far away from that atmosphere. Just a lady, a beautiful lady, a refined lady, amenable and unassuming.

SAMIA: Adil, this is no time for these glorious imaginings.

ADIL: Imaginings?

SAMIA: Of course, imaginings. After five years of marriage, don't you think I know what you are?

ADIL: And what am I?

SAMIA: Don't go on asking me that question every moment. Will you please note that I haven't yet had my bath, that I haven't done my hair, in fact haven't done a thing up until now except to talk nonsense with my respected husband. I haven't even lit the heater because you've refused to be serious and have just sat around chatting on the phone.

ADIL: God Almighty!

SAMIA (*motioning to him to go to the kitchen*): Do you mind?

ADIL (*making his way meekly to the kitchen*): Why trouble to say 'do you mind'? You know I'll comply with the order.

SAMIA: Of course I know that. (*She examines her hair in the mirror.*)

ADIL (*from offstage, in the kitchen*): Of course. I'm now in the kitchen turning on the Butagas for you.

SAMIA: Thank you. (*She goes to the heater in the bathroom and lights it as she hums to herself.*)

ADIL (*from offstage*): And the bottle of milk by the door – I'm taking it in and putting it on to heat. Any other orders?

Samia continues humming to herself.

ADIL (*entering, wiping his hands and singing*): The attainment of desires is not by hoping.

SAMIA (*going towards the bathroom door*): Adil, pass me the towel, will you?

ADIL (*passes her the towel*): The towel.

SAMIA: And the bathrobe too.

ADIL (*presenting her with the bathrobe*): And the bathrobe. You've
   got the soap and sponge?

SAMIA: The bottle of eau-de-Cologne please.

ADIL (*passing her the bottle*): And the eau-de-Cologne.

SAMIA: And the tin of powder.

Adil passes her the powder.

SAMIA: And now get out!

ADIL: I'm out!

*Samia closes the door of the bathroom and walks forward, humming
to herself, towards the bath. She no sooner looks inside it than she
lets out a scream.*

ADIL (*sitting with lowered head and then rising up in alarm at her
   scream*): What's wrong?

SAMIA (*opening the door of the bathroom and screaming*): Adil! Adil!
   Come quickly and look!

ADIL (*going towards the bathroom*): What is it? What's happened?

SAMIA (*pointing to the inside of the bath*): Look!

ADIL (*looks into the bath*): It's a cockroach.

SAMIA: Of course it's a cockroach, but how did it get in here?

ADIL: In the same way any cockroach gets into a house.

SAMIA: I mean here, into the tub, into the bath.

ADIL: Perhaps it fell from the ceiling.

SAMIA: The bath must be cleaned at once, but first it must be
   killed.

ADIL: Killed?

SAMIA: At once. You've got the insecticide in the kitchen.

ADIL: It's I who's going to be entrusted with killing it?

SAMIA: Of course.

ADIL: Of course, but look! It's going to come out by itself.

SAMIA: It would be better if it came out by itself because killing
   it in the bath will make a mess.

ADIL: Yes, it would be preferable if it were to come out nice and
   quietly so that it doesn't dirty the bath for you.

SAMIA: And when it comes out you can deal with it far away.

ADIL: Yes, far away from you.

SAMIA (*looking into the bath*): It doesn't look as if it will be able to.

ADIL (*looking closely*): It's trying.

SAMIA: It's slipping.

ADIL: The walls of the bath are slippery.

SAMIA: Yes, no sooner does it start climbing than it slips and falls.

ADIL: But it goes on trying.

SAMIA: And goes on again and again.

ADIL: With the same procedure.

SAMIA (*continuing to look*): Yes. Yes.

ADIL: Look, Samia. With all its strength it's climbing up the slippery wall.

SAMIA: And there it is slipping back again. There – it's fallen all the way back.

ADIL: And it's starting off to repeat the attempt.

SAMIA: Up it goes, up it goes. It's slipped! It's slipped! It's fallen!

ADIL: Don't you notice something, Samia?

SAMIA: What?

ADIL: That it's always at the same place.

SAMIA: Approximately a third of the way to the top of the bath.

ADIL: Yes, then it falls.

SAMIA: So it's unable to climb more than that.

ADIL: Because the walls of the bath are less steep near the bottom, which makes climbing easier. After that, though, it's straight up.

SAMIA: That's not the reason. Cockroaches can easily climb up a perpendicular wall, also along a ceiling. The reason is because it's slippery – no wall or ceiling is as slippery as this.

ADIL: How then can a cockroach climb up a wall of porcelain tiles, which is as slippery as this bath-tub?

SAMIA: And who told you that cockroaches can climb up a porcelain tile wall?

ADIL: Can't they?

SAMIA: Have you ever seen it?

ADIL: I rather imagined I had.

SAMIA: Imagined you had? So your lordship is imagining things!

ADIL: And you – have you seen it?

SAMIA: No, and so long as I have not seen a cockroach climbing up a wall of porcelain tiles I am unable to say that it could happen.

ADIL: Sounds logic.

SAMIA: Aren't you pleased with my logic?

ADIL: Did I say I wasn't? I was wondering, merely wondering. Is it impossible that something one hasn't seen with one's own eyes can happen?

SAMIA: Whoever said such a thing?

ADIL: I imagined you said something like that.

SAMIA: You imagined! Once again you're imagining things. Please don't imagine!

ADIL: As you say. I shall not imagine any more. As you wish me to be so positivistic, allow me to look in the dictionary.

SAMIA: Look for what?

ADIL: For the habits of cockroaches. Just a moment.

He hurries to the shelf of books by the bed and brings back a dictionary.

SAMIA: Hurry up, please.

ADIL (*turning over the pages*): Right away. Co . . . cock . . . cockroach, also known as black-beetle.

SAMIA: Black-beetle?

ADIL: Yes, black-beetle.

SAMIA: I prefer the word cockroach.

ADIL: I too.

SAMIA: What else does the dictionary say?

ADIL: The cockroach or black-beetle is a harmful insect that infests cloth, food, and paper. It is often found in lavatories and has long hairy horns or whiskers. It spoils more food than it actually requires as nourishment. It can live for about a year.

SAMIA: A year? It lives for a year?

ADIL: If it's not done away with and is left to enjoy its life.

SAMIA: Spoiling our food and clothes!

ADIL (*closing the dictionary*): That's all it says in the dictionary.

SAMIA: And now?

ADIL: And now what?

SAMIA: Are we going to go on like this looking at the cockroach?

ADIL: It's an enjoyable spectacle – don't you find it so?

SAMIA: What about the work we've got to do?

ADIL: Quite right – work.

SAMIA: We've got to put an end to it.

ADIL: And how do we put an end to it? This is something which is not in our hands.

SAMIA: In whose hands, then?

ADIL (*pointing to the cockroach*). In *its* hands. It's still climbing.

SAMIA: And also still falling.

ADIL: Yes, it climbs, then it rolls over, then it falls. Note the procedure: climbs, then slips, then rolls over, then falls to the bottom of the bath-tub.

SAMIA: It climbs, then slips, then rolls over, then falls to the bottom of the bath-tub.

ADIL: Exactly. Then it starts off again, without resting, without respite. It climbs . . .

SAMIA: Then it slips . . .

ADIL: Then it rolls over . . .

SAMIA: Then it falls . . .

ADIL: Then it climbs . . .

SAMIA: Listen, Adil – and then what?

ADIL: It hasn't had its final word.

SAMIA: I think that's plenty.

ADIL: Are you saying that to me?

SAMIA: Please, if you've got time to waste I haven't.

ADIL: Good God, and is that my fault?

SAMIA: Am I going to have my bath or aren't I?

ADIL: Go ahead! Have I stopped you?

SAMIA: And the cockroach?

ADIL: I am responsible only for myself.

SAMIA: Which means that you intend to leave it like this inside the bath?

ADIL: I think it's better to leave it as it is so that it can solve its problem by itself.

SAMIA: Are you joking, Adil? Is this a time for joking?

ADIL: On the contrary, I'm being extremely serious. Do you not see that it's still trying to save itself, so let's leave it to try.

SAMIA: Until when?

ADIL: We cannot – either you or I – decide when. That depends on its willpower – and up until now it has shown no intention of discontinuing its attempts. Look! So far it is showing no sign of being tired.

SAMIA: But I'm tired.

ADIL: Unfortunately.

SAMIA: And you? Aren't you tired?

ADIL: Of course, the same as you, but there's nothing to be done about it.

SAMIA: In short, I'm not having my bath today, or dressing, or going off to my job – all because of a cockroach which has fallen into the bath-tub and my solicitous husband who stands watching it and talking drivel.

ADIL: Thank you!

SAMIA: As one cannot depend upon you, I suppose I must act.

ADIL: What are you going to do?

SAMIA: Get the insecticide and look after things myself.

ADIL: You're going to destroy the cockroach?

SAMIA: Right away.

ADIL: Then go off and bring the insecticide.

SAMIA: I'll do just that.

> *Samia hurries off to the kitchen and Adil quickly locks the bathroom door from the inside. Samia, noting what has happened, turns back and raps at the locked door. Adil, inside the bathroom, moves towards the bath, humming to himself.*

SAMIA: What have you done, Adil? Open it!

> (*Adil does not reply to her: he is looking at the cockroach in the bath.*)

SAMIA: Have you done it, Adil?

ADIL (*pointing at the cockroach*): Up you go . . . up . . . up. Another step. Go on . . . go on . . .

SAMIA (*rapping at the door*): Adil, open it!

ADIL (*to the cockroach*): Stick to it! Stick to it! Struggle for your life!

SAMIA (*knocking vigorously*): I told you to open up, Adil. Open it! Can't you hear me?

ADIL (*to the cockroach*): They want to kill you with insecticide. Don't be afraid – I'll not open the door. Stick to it! Stick to it!

SAMIA (*rapping at the door*): Open the door, Adil! Open up, I tell you!

ADIL (*to the cockroach*): What a shame! You slipped, you rolled over and fell down as you do each time.

SAMIA (*rapping at the door*): Can't you hear all this knocking?

ADIL (*to the cockroach*): You want to have another go. Once again you're starting to climb. Why don't you rest a while? Rest for a moment, brother! Give yourself a breather? But what's the point? (*shouting*) There's no point!

SAMIA: No point? You say there's no point?

ADIL: Not to you!

SAMIA: So you've uttered at last! Are you going to open up eventually or not?

ADIL: No.

SAMIA: Are you saying no?

ADIL: Yes.

SAMIA: Are you saying no or yes?

ADIL: No and yes.

SAMIA: Speak intelligibly. Are you going to open up or not?

ADIL: I'll open up and I'll not open up.

SAMIA: Don't annoy me – define your attitude!

ADIL: You define yours!

SAMIA: Mine's clear – very clear.

ADIL: In relation to whom?

SAMIA: To you of course.

ADIL: I'm not asking about your attitude in relation to myself,
I'm asking about your attitude in relation to it.

SAMIA: What's it?

ADIL: The cockroach.

SAMIA: No, you've really gone mad! (*The telephone rings. She
hurries off to it and lifts up the receiver.*) Hullo. Who is it speaking?
Ah, good morning, Mr. Raafat. No, we're not dressed yet,
nor had breakfast, nor done a thing all morning – neither he
nor I. He spoke to you? Ah, it was he who rang you. I have,
in fact, noticed something strange about him: unnatural,
sick. Yes, he's in the bathroom. No, he's locked himself in.
A cockroach, my dear sir. Yes, an ordinary cockroach. No.
No. It's a long story. Yes, when we meet. No, I don't think
he's intending to go to work. I myself am late. Quite
definitely something's happened to him. No, don't you worry.
The company doctor? And what can the company doctor do?
I'm most grateful, Mr. Raafat. Where's Yusriyya? Good
morning, Yusriyya. Your husband noticed and told you? No,
don't you worry, Yusriyya. I'm very grateful to both you
and Mr. Raafat. Thank you. Thank you. (*She puts down the
receiver.*)

The cook enters; she is carrying the saucepan of milk.

COOK: Who put the milk on the fire and left it? The milk's all
boiled over on to the floor and the saucepan's quite empty.

SAMIA (*pointing to the bathroom*): It's his lordship.

COOK: And what's he been interfering in the kitchen for?

SAMIA: And why are *you* late today?

COOK: Transport.

SAMIA: Jam packed, not even a place to stand, isn't that so?
COOK: Exactly.
SAMIA: I know your excuse, know it in advance!
COOK: Shall I prepare the breakfast?
SAMIA: Breakfast? You'd better wait till we see where it's all
    going to end. (*She points at the bathroom.*)
COOK (*looking towards the bathroom*): It's him?
SAMIA: Yes, inside – he's locked himself in.
COOK: Why? I hope nothing's wrong.
SAMIA: The cockroach.
COOK: Cockroach?
SAMIA: Look here, Umm Attiya, did you clean the bath well
    yesterday?
COOK: Of course, Ma'am – with carbolic acid.
SAMIA: Impossible.
COOK: The bottle's along by the kitchen.
SAMIA: You're sure?
COOK: I swear to you.
SAMIA: Then where's this wretched cockroach come from?
COOK: From the skylight, from the stairs, from the pipes, from
    out of the cracks in the walls – however much you clean a
    house it's bound to have cockroaches and ants.

*All this time Adil has been in the bathroom engrossed in watching
the cockroach. He makes gestures to it as he follows it climbing up
and falling down; by sighs and miming he expresses all his emotions
and concern.*

SAMIA (*suddenly shouting*): Oh, and where's it all going to end? My
    poor nerves! My poor nerves!
COOK: Shall I bring you a cup of tea?
SAMIA: No, you go about your work and let me be for the moment.
COOK: The insecticide's along by the kitchen, Ma'am. I'll bring
    it and . . .
SAMIA: I know the insecticide's in the kitchen but the trouble is
    . . . Off you go and let me alone, Umm Attiya – I know what
    I'm about.
COOK: As you say, Ma'am. (*She goes out.*)
SAMIA (*going towards the bathroom and rapping at the door*): Listen,
    Adil, I want to have a few words with you. Are you listening?
ADIL (*without moving or interrupting his watching of the cockroach*): I'm
    listening.

SAMIA: I think things have gone on quite long enough.

ADIL (*automatically echoing her words*): Long enough.

SAMIA: And there's a limit to one's patience.

ADIL: One's patience.

SAMIA: And my nerves are in ribbons.

ADIL: In ribbons.

SAMIA: And you're behaving ridiculously.

ADIL: Ridiculously.

SAMIA (*shouting*): This is unbearable! Won't you answer me? Answer anything! Answer! Answer! Answer!

ADIL: Answer! Answer! Answer!

SAMIA (*leaving the bathroom door in despair*): It's hopeless! There's no longer any point in speaking to that creature. He just repeats my words like a parrot. We've now got a cockroach and a parrot in the bathroom!

COOK (*entering*): Today you're both later than usual, Ma'am.

SAMIA: Of course.

COOK: Today's a holiday?

SAMIA: It's not a holiday or anything of the sort – it's a working day as usual.

COOK: All right but . . .

SAMIA: But what? His lordship's locked himself up in the bathroom and doesn't want to open it, nor does he want to answer me. I've given up knocking and trying to talk to him. I've come to the end of my tether with him . . . there's no way of making contact with him.

COOK: Seeing that he's bolted himself in . . .

SAMIA: There's only one way.

COOK: Let's try it.

SAMIA: Do you know what it is?

COOK: No.

SAMIA: Break down the door.

COOK: Break down the bathroom door?

SAMIA: Yes.

COOK: And who's going to do that?

SAMIA: Can't you?

COOK: Me?

SAMIA: Certainly, you'd not be able to.

COOK: It's a solid door and would need a carpenter . . .

SAMIA: Go and fetch a carpenter.

COOK: There's no carpenter near-by in the district.

SAMIA: What's to be done?

COOK: Leave it in the hands of the Almighty. We'll let him be for a while until he gets fed up and opens up of his own accord.

SAMIA: He won't get fed up. So long as that wretched thing's got a breath of life in it.

COOK: But he'll have to come out so as to go to work.

SAMIA: He'll forget work or pretend to. I know him – sometimes he forgets himself. Many times he's unable to get any control over himself or over his time.

COOK: And your own work, Ma'am?

SAMIA: That's the trouble. I can't go without him because they'll ask me about him. What shall I say to them? Shall I say that he hasn't turned up to work because he's engrossed in watching a cockroach in the bath?

COOK: Say that he's tired, indisposed.

SAMIA: They'll immediately send round the company doctor.

COOK: Let him come and good luck to him!

SAMIA: And if he examines him and finds he's not indisposed at all?

COOK: That's true.

SAMIA: He's always getting me into such embarrassing situations. If I weren't always alongside him to rescue him and guide him he'd get into any number of scrapes.

COOK: May the Almighty keep you and give you strength!

SAMIA: He always yields to me, he never disobeys me.

COOK: That's evident.

SAMIA: What's happened to him then this morning? I said to him: Open up! Open up! but he seemed stone-deaf.

COOK: All his life he's paid attention to what you have to say.

SAMIA: Except for today. I don't know what's happened to him.

COOK: Somebody's put the evil eye on him.

SAMIA: And where will be the end of it?

COOK: Be patient, Ma'am. Patience is a virtue.

SAMIA: My patience has run out, it's finished, it's had it!

COOK (*looking in the direction of the bathroom*): But you mean to say that all he's doing is just watching a cockroach?

SAMIA: You don't believe it?

COOK: Honestly, Ma'am, if it weren't that I believe every word you say I'd not make head or tail of it.

SAMIA: Of course – this wouldn't happen with a normal man.

COOK: Shall I speak to him, Ma'am?

SAMIA: You?

COOK: I'll have a go.

SAMIA: Go on!

*The cook knocks on the bathroom door. Adil, motionless, is still
watching what is going on in the bath-tub.*

COOK (*she knocks again, then again and again, and finally shouts out*):
   I'm Umm Attiya.
ADIL (*raising his head*): Umm Attiya? What do you want?
COOK: To wash the bathroom floor.
ADIL: It's forbidden.
COOK: Forbidden?
ADIL: Today it's forbidden.
COOK: I'll bring a new piece of soap for the bath.
ADIL: There's soap here.
COOK: A clean towel?
ADIL: There is one. There's everything.
COOK: Don't you need anything?
ADIL: All I need is for you to take yourself off and shut up.
COOK: Just as you say.

The cook returns despondently to Samia.

SAMIA: I told you it was no good.
COOK: You're quite right.
SAMIA: So what's to be done? One's got to do something, one's
   simply got to.
COOK: Calm down, Ma'am, and leave things to the Almighty!
SAMIA: One can't just shut up about it – one can't!

*She walks nervously about the room, while the cook watches her and
sighs. There is a ring at the door.*

COOK: It's the front door!
SAMIA: Who could it be?
COOK: I'll go and see. (*She goes out.*)
SAMIA (*standing up and listening, then calling out*): Who is it, Umm
   Attiya?
COOK (*entering in a state of flurry*): It's the doctor, Ma'am!
SAMIA: Doctor? What doctor?
COOK: He said he was the company doctor. I put him in the
   lounge.
SAMIA: The company doctor? Ah, no doubt Raafat sent him,

thinking that the situation demanded it. And now what's to be done? This is just what I feared. (*She moves towards the bathroom door and knocks.*) Adil! Open up, Adil – there's something very important.

ADIL (*his gaze directed at the inside of the bath*): I know – very important.

SAMIA: The situation's critical.

ADIL: No doubt about it. (*He points to the cockroach in the bath.*) Its situation is indeed critical, and you know its situation is critical.

SAMIA: Whose situation? I'm talking about your situation.

ADIL: That also is only too well known.

SAMIA: Open up, Adil. Open up so I can explain the situation to you.

ADIL: The situation's clear and requires no explaining.

SAMIA: You're wrong, something new's occurred: the doctor's come.

ADIL: Doctor? You've brought a doctor? – to do away with this poor thing? An entomologist of course?

SAMIA: Entomologist? What are you talking about? The doctor's come about you. Open up – the doctor's here for you.

ADIL: For me? An entomologist?

SAMIA: What entomologist, Adil? The company doctor; the company doctor's come to examine you.

ADIL (*jumping to his feet*): What's that you're saying?

SAMIA: Open up and I'll explain to you.

ADIL (*realizing what she's up to*): Open up? Not likely! I've heard that one before!

SAMIA: I'm not fooling, Adil, and I'm not playing a trick. I'm talking seriously: the company doctor has arrived and is in the lounge. It seems Raafat sent him thinking you were ill.

ADIL: Me ill?

SAMIA: So Raafat understood, and the doctor's actually come.

ADIL: If he's actually come, why don't I hear his voice?

SAMIA: He's in the lounge. I told you he was in the lounge – and please don't make him wait any longer!

ADIL: In short, you want me to open up?

SAMIA: Of course, in order to be able to deal with the question of the doctor.

ADIL: Cut this story of the doctor out!

SAMIA: Don't you believe he's here?

ADIL: If he's really come for me, let him speak to me himself.

SAMIA: You want him to come in here?

ADIL: Isn't that the normal thing?

SAMIA: All right. (*She calls out.*) Umm Attiya – ask the doctor to come in here.

COOK: Certainly, Ma'am.

Samia hurriedly arranges her hair and clothes preparatory to meeting the doctor.

COOK (*at the door*): Please, in here, Doctor.

SAMIA (*meeting him*): Please come in, Doctor.

DOCTOR (*enters carrying a small bag*): Good morning.

SAMIA: Good morning. It seems we've put you out for no . . .

DOCTOR: Not at all. I was already dressed and was about to leave when Mr. Raafat contacted me by telephone. I came along immediately – my house is just near-by.

SAMIA: We are extremely grateful but . . .

DOCTOR: And how does Mr. Adil feel?

SAMIA: The fact is he's . . .

DOCTOR: In any event everything will become clear when I've examined him. Where is he, might I ask?

SAMIA: He's . . . he's . . . he's here in the bathroom. I'll call him.

DOCTOR: Let him take his bath in peace.

SAMIA: He's not taking a bath. He's . . . just a moment. (*She knocks at the bathroom door.*) Adil! Open up, Adil – the doctor's waiting.

ADIL: Where is he?

SAMIA: Here in the room. Answer him, Doctor!

DOCTOR: Mr. Adil!

ADIL: Good God! It's true!

DOCTOR (*to Samia*): What's he saying?

SAMIA (*to Adil*): You believe me? Now open up!

ADIL (*opening the door of the bathroom and standing by it*): Doctor? Truly I'm most embarrassed . . .

DOCTOR: How are you now, Mr. Adil?

ADIL: I? I'm fine.

DOCTOR: Fine?

ADIL: Naturally.

SAMIA: But he felt slightly unwell early this morning.

ADIL: I?

SAMIA: Of course you. Since early this morning you haven't been feeling right.

ADIL: And you know the reason why?

SAMIA: Whatever the reason, the doctor's come and there's an end to it. In any case you're late for work and there's no harm in the doctor giving you a day off, isn't that so, Doctor?

DOCTOR: Before prescribing anything I must make an examination. Please lie down on the bed, Mr. Adil.

ADIL: But I . . .

SAMIA: Listen to what the doctor has to say, Adil, and let him examine you.

ADIL: Examine? And say it appears . . .

SAMIA: Anyway, you're run down.

ADIL: But that's not sufficient reason . . .

SAMIA: It's enough for now.

ADIL: I prefer him to know the real reason.

SAMIA: The real reason?

ADIL: Yes, come along, Doctor.

DOCTOR: Where to?

ADIL (*drawing him towards the bathroom*): In here.

SAMIA: You're mad, Adil! (*She draws the doctor away from the bathroom.*) Please, Doctor, come away.

ADIL: Leave him alone, Samia. Let me tell him of the real reason. (*Pulls the doctor towards him.*) Come along, Doctor.

SAMIA: Don't listen to him, Doctor. (*Pulls the doctor towards her.*) Come along.

DOCTOR (*at a loss, being pulled in opposite directions by the two of them*): Please! Please!

SAMIA: Let the doctor go, Adil. It's not right.

ADIL: You let him go!

SAMIA: Allow him to examine you – that's what he's come for.

ADIL: No, I'll tell him the real reason.

SAMIA: But that won't . . . won't . . .

ADIL: It must be done.

SAMIA: You don't realize what you're doing. Come here, Doctor, please. (*She pulls him.*)

ADIL: But the doctor is interested to know what it is I want to show him. I'm sure of that. Please, Doctor, listen to what I have to say. Come along! (*He pulls at the doctor.*)

DOCTOR: Excuse me! Excuse me! (*He tries to release himself from the two of them.*)

SAMIA: I'm sorry, Doctor, but my husband Adil doesn't appreciate . . .

ADIL: Doesn't appreciate what? In what way don't I appreciate?
    I know exactly what I'm doing. My mind's quite made up.
SAMIA: I've warned you, Adil, I've warned you.
ADIL: I'll take the responsibility.
SAMIA: All right, you're free to do as you please.
DOCTOR (*bewildered*): What's it all about? Please – tell me.
ADIL (*drawing him into the bathroom*): Come along with me,
    Doctor, and I'll explain things to you.
DOCTOR (*in astonishment*): Where to?
ADIL (*standing in front of the bath*): Here, look! What do you see
    inside the bath-tub?
DOCTOR (*looking*): Nothing. There's no water in it.
ADIL: Of course there's no water in it, but isn't there something
    else?
DOCTOR: No, nothing – it's empty.
ADIL: Yet even so, there is something there.
DOCTOR: Something? Such as?
ADIL: Do you find it absolutely sparkling white?
DOCTOR: Yes, absolutely.
ADIL: But you can't say that it's absolutely clean.
DOCTOR: Who am I to criticize your cleanliness?
ADIL: Thank you for your kind words but the obvious truth of
    the matter is that there is something dirty in the bath.
SAMIA: So you've admitted it's dirty and must be done away with?
ADIL: Dirty's something and doing away with it is something else.
DOCTOR (*looks at them both uncomprehendingly*): If you'll allow me . . .
ADIL: Look down here into the bath, Doctor, and you'll
    understand.

The doctor looks down with great attention.

ADIL: Do you not see something moving?
DOCTOR (*without interest*): A cockroach.
ADIL: A cockroach? Well done!
DOCTOR: And so?
ADIL: This cockroach is the very core and essence.
DOCTOR: Very core and essence?
ADIL: Look at it well, Doctor. What do you notice about it?
DOCTOR: From what point of view?
ADIL: From the point of view of its behaviour.
DOCTOR: Its behaviour?
SAMIA: Keep quiet, Adil – let me explain to the doctor.

ADIL: No, please, Samia – let me do the speaking.

SAMIA: And why should I not speak? At least I won't tell it wrong.

ADIL: And I'll tell it wrong?

SAMIA: Don't complicate things for me. Let me do the talking, because I'm better than you at explaining things.

ADIL: Of course, but it's only I who . . .

SAMIA: Today you're opposing me all along the line in a quite unreasonable way.

ADIL: It's not opposition. I didn't mean . . . it's just . . .

SAMIA: Just what? Listen, Doctor . . .

ADIL: A moment, Samia, please! Let me speak first because I've got my own point of view.

SAMIA: And I too have a point of view.

ADIL: Of course. Of course – and your point of view is respected, very respected. But allow me a minute, one single minute and no more.

SAMIA: No, not even half a minute.

ADIL: Please, Samia.

SAMIA: Out of the question.

ADIL: Samia!

DOCTOR: Friends, there's no reason for all this disagreement. Explain to me first of all exactly what the problem's all about.

SAMIA: The problem, Doctor . . .

ADIL: For which of us did the Doctor come? Was it not for me? Tell me, Doctor, for whom did you come here?

DOCTOR: For you.

ADIL: For me, then it is I who shall explain to you . . .

DOCTOR: You or the lady – the important thing is for me to know what it's about.

SAMIA: Do you hear, Adil: you or I, and as I'm the woman I have priority.

ADIL: Heavens! Even in this, even in my own illness?

SAMIA: You've now admitted you're ill.

ADIL: In the doctor's view. Of course he has come because there's an ill person in the house, and the ill person is supposed to be me, but the fact, Doctor, is . . .

SAMIA: The fact is that he's . . .

ADIL: The fact is that I'm . . .

SAMIA (*violently*): Whatever next, Adil? Please, don't force me to . . .

ADIL: It's my fault, my fault as usual, because it's always my fault.

DOCTOR: The important thing, friends, is: what's it all about?

SAMIA: I'm sorry, Doctor – we're taking up too much of your time.

DOCTOR: No, not at all, only I'd like to understand . . .

SAMIA: You'll understand, Doctor, you'll understand – if he'd just shut up for a moment I'd be able to explain to you.

ADIL: Just the opposite.

SAMIA: What's just the opposite?

ADIL: If I keep silent he'll not understand what it's about.

SAMIA: Meaning that I'm incapable of making him understand, or do you mean I'm a liar and will falsify the facts?

ADIL: God forbid! Would I ever insinuate such a thing!

DOCTOR: Allow me, so as to put an end to all disagreement, just let me find out what it's about by myself. Please, Mr. Adil, please lie down on the bed so that I can examine you and then I'll know the truth for myself.

ADIL: No, Doctor – the truth's not to be found on the bed but in the bath.

DOCTOR: In the bath?

ADIL: Yes, in this bath – this cockroach.

DOCTOR: Permit me, please excuse me, but I . . . I don't understand anything at all.

SAMIA: It's not his fault – of course he can't understand.

ADIL: I'll explain the matter in a few words – listen, Doctor, look carefully at this cockroach and tell me what it's doing now?

DOCTOR (looking into the bath): What's it doing? It's doing nothing.

ADIL: Look carefully, Doctor.

DOCTOR: What are you getting at exactly?

SAMIA: What Adil is getting at is that . . .

ADIL: No, no, let the doctor discover it for himself.

DOCTOR (looking intently into the bath): Discover?

ADIL: Don't you see, for example, that the cockroach is trying to do something?

DOCTOR: Of course, it's trying to get out of the bath.

ADIL: Marvellous! Marvellous! We've got there.

DOCTOR (looking at him): Where have we got?

ADIL: To the heart of the whole matter.

DOCTOR (nodding his head): Understood. Understood. It's all quite clear now.

ADIL: You understand what I'm driving at, Doctor? This is the point of departure and I shall explain my attitude to you.

DOCTOR: No, no, there's no need to explain – I've understood.

(*He goes out of the bathroom and whispers to Samia*) Might I have a word with you?

SAMIA (*following him*): Of course, Doctor, go ahead.

DOCTOR (*whispering*): He's really overdoing it. How many hours does he work at the factory?

SAMIA: The usual hours, but there's something else to it.

DOCTOR: Does he do other work?

SAMIA: He is preparing a thesis for his doctorate, but this condition of his . . .

DOCTOR: Understood, Understood. He's certainly in need of rest. I'll write down for him all that's necessary. Would you allow me, Mr. Adil?

ADIL (*coming out of the bathroom*): What, Doctor?

DOCTOR: Nothing – it's just that having visited you at home in my capacity of company doctor, I must examine you, if only for the purpose of establishing that I've been here.

ADIL: But I'm not ill.

DOCTOR: I know that, but I am required to put in a report and the report must show that an examination has been made.

ADIL: You came in an official capacity?

DOCTOR: Of course.

ADIL: Ah, in that case I must help you. However, what are you going to write in your report seeing that I'm not ill?

DOCTOR: Leave things to me. First of all, would you just lie down here on the bed.

ADIL: I've put on weight these last years.

DOCTOR: That's obvious – you're getting flabby before your time.

SAMIA: He's grown himself a real paunch!

ADIL: From fatty food – Umm Attiya's cooking!

DOCTOR: Maybe also from lack of exercise.

ADIL: I've got no time for exercise.

DOCTOR: You overdo things at work.

ADIL: I have to.

DOCTOR (*examining his chest and back with the stethoscope*): Take a deep breath. Enough, Enough. Do you smoke?

ADIL: A little.

DOCTOR: Drink a lot of coffee?

ADIL: A couple of cups a day.

DOCTOR: Alcohol? Drugs?

ADIL: No, no. Never, never.

DOCTOR: You naturally sometimes stay up late at night.

ADIL: Sometimes, when my work requires me to, but in any case it's never later than midnight.

DOCTOR: Do you sleep well?

ADIL: Like a log.

DOCTOR: Do you have unpleasant dreams?

ADIL: Neither pleasant nor unpleasant, I don't dream at all.

DOCTOR: Perhaps you dream and don't remember your dreams.

ADIL: Maybe.

DOCTOR: You don't suffer from anything unusual?

ADIL: No, not at all.

DOCTOR: Thank you.

The doctor sets about writing out his prescription to one side of the room.

SAMIA (*approaching the doctor*): I hope everything's all right, Doctor?

DOCTOR: Fine, everything's just fine – he's in splendid health, thanks be to God. There's not a thing wrong with him. I'll write him out a prescription for some tranquillizers and give him three days' sick leave.

SAMIA: Three days?

DOCTOR: Too little?

SAMIA: No, it's a lot, too much.

ADIL (*jumping to his feet*): What's too much?

SAMIA: The doctor wants to give you three days' sick leave.

ADIL: Three days?

SAMIA: One day's plenty, Doctor.

ADIL: Of course one day, and there wasn't even any reason to have today off if it hadn't been that you came, Doctor – so as to justify your coming here.

DOCTOR: As you say – one day, my dear sir.

ADIL: Thank you, Doctor.

DOCTOR: On condition that you stay in bed.

ADIL: Stay in bed?

DOCTOR: It's necessary.

ADIL: And what's the necessity?

DOCTOR: For complete rest and relaxation.

ADIL: And if I find complete rest and relaxation somewhere else?

DOCTOR: Where?

ADIL: In the bathroom, for example?

SAMIA: Do you hear, Doctor? He'll be spending the day in the bathroom.

DOCTOR: There's no harm in his taking a warm bath, it'll help him to relax.

SAMIA: He'll not be taking a bath at all, neither warm nor cold.

DOCTOR: What, then, will he do in the bathroom?

SAMIA: Ask him.

ADIL: I shall watch the cockroach. What's wrong with that?

SAMIA: You've heard with your very own ears, haven't you, Doctor?

DOCTOR: The cockroach? Again?

ADIL: Come along to the bath with me and I'll explain things to you.

DOCTOR (looking at his watch): Another time, it's getting late and I've got some urgent work to do.

ADIL: My explanation will take no more than a minute.

DOCTOR: I promise to visit you again shortly when, God willing, your nerves will have calmed down.

ADIL: My nerves are perfectly calm. I would have liked you to stay for a while so that . . .

DOCTOR: I'll come back. I'll come back.

ADIL: When?

DOCTOR: In the afternoon. In the afternoon.

ADIL: When you return in the afternoon everything will have changed.

DOCTOR: What will have changed?

ADIL: The cockroach will – will have been destroyed. Do you think my wife will leave things as they are?

SAMIA: Of course not. You can't stop me from using the bath the whole day – it's unreasonable.

ADIL (to the doctor): Do you hear?

SAMIA: Judge, Doctor! Don't I have to go off to my work at the factory? Hasn't his lordship already made me late enough?

ADIL: Doctor, it's not I who've made her late. Her being late has another reason. Ask her about it!

SAMIA: What's the other reason?

ADIL: Your insistence on taking a bath today.

SAMIA: Ask him, Doctor, what the reason was for my not taking a bath today.

ADIL: I'll tell you the reason, Doctor: the reason is that she wants to destroy this cockroach.

SAMIA: There you are, Doctor!

DOCTOR: The fact is that the question . . .

ADIL: I'm certain, Doctor, you'll come down on the side of truth, for the question is clear.

SAMIA: Of course it's clear, but don't try to influence the doctor. He understands everything.

ADIL: I'm not trying to influence the doctor. It's you who from the very beginning were trying to influence him, but he understands perfectly my purpose.

SAMIA: Your purpose?

ADIL: Of course.

SAMIA: Tell us, Doctor: have you really understood anything of him?

ADIL: And have you understood anything of her, Doctor?

SAMIA: Answer, Doctor!

ADIL: Yes, answer!

DOCTOR (*at a loss between the two of them*): The truth of the matter is I . . . is I . . .

ADIL: Listen, Doctor; the essence of the matter can be put into a few words: put yourself in the same position.

DOCTOR: Your position?

ADIL: The position of the cockroach.

DOCTOR (*hurriedly taking up his bag*): No – please excuse me.

He rushes out with Samia and Adil in his wake calling out to him.

SAMIA: Wait, Doctor!

ADIL: Just a moment, Doctor!

CURTAIN

Act Three – The Fate of the Cockroach

The same scene less than a minute later. Samia and Adil are returning to the room after the doctor's hasty departure.

ADIL: Why did the doctor leave like that?

SAMIA: Ask yourself.

ADIL: Ask myself? Why? Did I do anything wrong?

SAMIA: You? From the moment you woke up this morning you haven't stopped doing things wrong.

ADIL: Good Heavens!

SAMIA: We woke up in the morning in fine shape, got ourselves ready to go out to work, and then your lordship causes us all this unnecessary delay.

ADIL: It's I who've caused it?

SAMIA: Your cockroach!

ADIL: And was it I who placed it in the bath?

SAMIA: What it amounts to is that you've got the day off – official sick leave. As for me, I've got to go off to my work. It's true I'm late but I'll make the best of it and give as an excuse your being ill and the company doctor coming to the house.

The doctor reappears.

DOCTOR: Please excuse me! I went off in a most impolite manner.

ADIL: No, don't mention it, Doctor.

DOCTOR: I was afraid I'd be late for my other work. On thinking it over, though, I feel that my prime duty lies here. I have therefore returned quickly to ask that I might continue my examination of the case.

SAMIA: Thank you, Doctor.

DOCTOR: I'd like to have a word in private with your wife – would you allow me, Mr. Adil?

ADIL: Of course. Of course. I'll go into the bathroom.

DOCTOR: Take your time!

Adil goes into the bathroom and locks the door on himself. He goes back to watching the bath with interest. He makes signs and gestures as he follows the cockroach's movements, like someone following a game of chess.

SAMIA: Is anything wrong, Doctor?

DOCTOR: I want to ask you about certain things.

SAMIA: Go ahead!

DOCTOR: My questions will perhaps be a trifle embarrassing in that they may touch upon some personal aspects, but my duty as a practising doctor demands that I do so. May I put my questions?

SAMIA: Of course, Doctor, go ahead!

DOCTOR: What's your opinion about your husband's personality?

SAMIA: In what respect?

DOCTOR: In respect of strength and weakness.

SAMIA: In relation to whom?

DOCTOR: In relation to yourself of course.

SAMIA: I . . . I believe his personality to be weaker than mine.

DOCTOR: Does he know it?

SAMIA: Certainly.

DOCTOR: He has told you so openly?

SAMIA: No, but he believes it deep inside him.

DOCTOR: How do you know?

SAMIA: He is always stating that I boss him and make him obey my orders and tyrannize him.

DOCTOR: Tyrannize him?

SAMIA: That's what he says.

DOCTOR: Then he believes or imagines that you are tyrannizing him?

SAMIA: Yes.

DOCTOR: My diagnosis is appropriate.

SAMIA: What diagnosis?

DOCTOR: This question of the cockroach.

SAMIA: And what's the connection?

DOCTOR: You want to do away with the cockroach and he wants to save it from your hands.

SAMIA: You mean, Doctor . . .

DOCTOR: Yes, in his inner consciousness he has identified himself with the cockroach, and this is the secret of his concern and affection for it.

SAMIA: Extraordinary! D'you think so, Doctor?

DOCTOR: There can be no other reason.

SAMIA: But . . .

DOCTOR: This is a very obvious example from modern psychology. I am not a specialist in psychiatry, but I have made a private study of it as a hobby and I am indeed lucky to have come across this case today.

SAMIA: Are you certain it's a psychological state?

DOCTOR: A typical case.

SAMIA: Can it be treated?

DOCTOR: The treatment is easy, extremely easy.

SAMIA: Whatever you order me to do I shall carry out immediately.

DOCTOR: The treatment requires no more than your persuading your husband that there is no similarity between him and the cockroach.

SAMIA: And how shall I persuade him?

DOCTOR: That's the problem.

SAMIA: A way must be found.

DOCTOR: First of all you must on your side show affection for the cockroach.

SAMIA: Show affection for the cockroach?

DOCTOR: That's essential, because any hurt done by you to the cockroach would, in your husband's view, be a hurt done to him personally.

SAMIA: But this is madness.

DOCTOR: Naturally – it's a pathological condition.

SAMIA: But he's perfectly sane. Up until this morning he could not have been more balanced in all his behaviour, performing his company work perfectly well.

DOCTOR: He is in fact extremely well balanced and will always be able to perform his company work in the best possible manner, of that I'm sure.

SAMIA: Then he's a normal person.

DOCTOR: Normal in all things except one – that of the cockroach.

SAMIA: That's right, no sooner is the cockroach mentioned than . . .

DOCTOR: Than he begins to speak and act strangely.

SAMIA: That is so.

DOCTOR: Yet even so there's no cause for worry. With a little wisdom and patience, kindness and adjustment, we shall quickly be able to sort things out for the best.

SAMIA: You may be confident, Doctor, that I shall employ both wisdom and patience and shall be kind and compliant with him in everything he wants.

DOCTOR: That is all that is now required, so let's begin trying.

SAMIA: Yes, we shall try.

DOCTOR: First of all, we must go along and participate in what he's doing.

SAMIA (*she goes with the doctor behind her and gently knocks on the bathroom door*): Adil!

ADIL (*getting to his feet and opening the door to them*): Have you finished your little private talk?

SAMIA: Yes, the doctor was advising me . . .

DOCTOR: To put you on a special diet. I'd like you to be a little slimmer.

ADIL: Slimmer? Me?

DOCTOR: Why not? Do you want to let your body get flabby?

ADIL: Has my wife complained about my physique?

DOCTOR: No, I'm talking medically – an increase in weight leads to lethargy, and you are in need of energy.

ADIL: I'm exceedingly energetic, extremely energetic, which can be seen from the fact that I wake up in the morning before the alarm goes off. Ask Samia.

SAMIA: Quite correct.

DOCTOR: Then you admit your husband possesses this quality.

SAMIA: No doubt about it – he's exceedingly energetic.

DOCTOR: Do you hear that, Mr. Adil? Your wife is being very complimentary about you.

ADIL: She can't deny I'm energetic, though of course I'm not as energetic as this cockroach.

DOCTOR: The cockroach? Ah, yes, of course.

ADIL: Look, Doctor. Look, Samia. It's still struggling – with the same perseverance. I tried to catch it out slacking or giving up, but never . . . never . . . never.

SAMIA (*looking into the bath-tub with feigned interest*): It's certainly courageous.

ADIL: And what courage!

SAMIA: I've begun to love it.

ADIL (*looking at her*): Love it?

SAMIA: Yes, doesn't its courage deserve love?

ADIL: You wanted to destroy it with insecticide.

SAMIA: I was stupid.

ADIL: Thanks be to God!

SAMIA: Look at its whiskers – they're beautiful!

ADIL: Whose whiskers?

SAMIA: The cockroach's of course.

ADIL: Its whiskers are beautiful?

SAMIA: Don't you think so?

ADIL: You making fun of me?

SAMIA: Of you? No, no – I swear to you, Adil. Please don't be angry. I swear to you I'm not making fun of you. I'm being absolutely serious now. I'm sincere in what I say, and when I say that its whiskers please me, be sure that I really mean it.

ADIL: And since when did you discover its whiskers were so beautiful?

SAMIA: Since . . . since a moment ago when I looked carefully at it.

ADIL: I myself have been looking carefully at it from early morning and can't find anything beautiful about it.

SAMIA: You're being modest.

ADIL: Modest? Me? What's the connection?

SAMIA: Oh none, none at all.

DOCTOR: Certainly there's no connection whatsoever.

SAMIA: Of course, Adil, be sure there's no connection.

ADIL (looking at the two of them): What's all this confusion about?

SAMIA: Nothing at all, Adil – everything's quite in order. All that's happened is that the doctor and I have come to understand your point of view completely.

DOCTOR: Certainly. Certainly.

ADIL (doubting them): And what is my point of view?

SAMIA: It's – it's that this cockroach . . .

DOCTOR: Should not come to any harm.

SAMIA: Yes. Yes.

ADIL: Do you know why?

SAMIA: We know all right.

ADIL: No, Samia, I'm certain you don't really know. I shall explain it to you and the doctor.

SAMIA: No, there's no need, Adil, no need at all. We know and appreciate the position. God willing, everything will return to normal with a little wisdom and patience.

ADIL: Yes, a little patience. All that's wanted is a little patience, because things may go on for a while. In any case, it's both interesting and exciting. I don't get bored watching, and so long as this cockroach goes on putting up such a struggle to get out of its impasse, it is not right that we should destroy it.

SAMIA: Who said we were going to destroy it? On the contrary, Adil, I'll look after it with every care. I'll sacrifice myself for it.

ADIL: Sacrifice yourself for it? Please, Samia – there's no need to make fun.

SAMIA: Absolutely not, Adil. What can I do to convince you that I'm definitely not making fun?

ADIL: When all's said and done, the struggle this cockroach is putting up stirs within me a feeling of respect.

SAMIA: And who said we had less respect for it than you? We are at one with you, Adil – absolutely at one. Maybe we have even more respect and appreciation for it than you, isn't that so, Doctor?

DOCTOR: Of course. Of course.

ADIL: More than me? No, I don't think so.

SAMIA: And why not?

ADIL: Because I've been watching it since early morning, following its every movement. It amazes me the amount of strength that's stored up in it – quite remarkable strength.

SAMIA: I'm in agreement with you about that, Adil, and I really do find that it has an extraordinarily strong personality.

ADIL: Strong personality?

SAMIA: Don't you think so?

ADIL: I think it's an exaggeration to say it's got a personality.

SAMIA: Honestly, Adil, it's got a strong personality – you must believe that.

ADIL: Listen, Samia – don't get characteristics mixed up. The fact that a cockroach has such strength and determination is both acceptable and reasonable, but to say it's got a personality is going too far.

SAMIA: I insist it has got a personality. Maybe even its personality is stronger than mine – wouldn't you agree with me there, Doctor?

DOCTOR: Very likely.

ADIL: What's very likely, Doctor? That this cockroach's personality is stronger than Samia's?

DOCTOR: Don't, Mr. Adil, overestimate the personality of your lady wife – with all due deference to her.

ADIL: I'm not overestimating but – but to compare my wife with a cockroach!

SAMIA: But I'm in agreement, Adil.

ADIL: It's not a question of whether you're in agreement or not in agreement – we're talking about the comparison itself.

SAMIA: And why should we reject the comparison, seeing that the cockroach commands respect? It does me honour.

ADIL: Are we back again at making fun?

SAMIA: Not at all, I swear to you, Adil. I'm absolutely serious – just ask the doctor.

ADIL: Listen, Samia, when words lose their normal dimensions, then everything loses its seriousness. I've begun to feel that you're in league with the doctor to ridicule my ideas.

DOCTOR: God forbid, Mr. Adil!

SAMIA: No, Adil, please don't make such an accusation against the doctor. He is the last person to wish to harm your self-respect. He hasn't interrupted his other work and devoted all his time to us in order to make fun of you and your ideas.

DOCTOR: On the contrary, the . . . the fact of the matter is that I . . .

SAMIA: Don't say anything, Doctor – it's obvious what your feelings are.

ADIL: I'm sorry – I no doubt misunderstood.

SAMIA: Be sure, Adil, that we are of the same opinion as you. There is now no disagreement between us. The cockroach is as much an object of affection to us as to you.

ADIL: Affection?

SAMIA: Yes, and in deference to it and to you I have decided not to have a bath today in order to prove to you I won't attempt to harm it.

ADIL: Thank you.

SAMIA: Doesn't that please you?

ADIL: Of course it pleases me.

SAMIA: Everything that pleases you, Adil, everything that makes you happy, I shall at once put into effect for you.

ADIL: What's all this tenderness about?

SAMIA: I regret all my hasty actions.

ADIL: What hasty actions?

SAMIA: I haven't always been nice to you.

ADIL: That is your right as a woman and a wife, but it is my duty as a man and a husband to endure.

SAMIA: No, from now on you shall not endure, I shall not make you endure.

ADIL: What's happened now? What's come over the universe?

DOCTOR: Your wife is one of the best of wives, Mr. Adil, and is blindly obedient to you.

ADIL: Since when?

SAMIA: Since today.

ADIL: And why today?

SAMIA: Because it . . . because I . . .

DOCTOR: Because she naturally doesn't want to see you being ill.

ADIL: But I'm not ill.

DOCTOR: Of course. Of course you're not ill at all.

SAMIA: What the doctor means is you're . . .

DOCTOR: Certainly. What I mean is that it's clear you're not ill.
That was established by examining you, be sure of that.
However, the whole object is to remove the *idea* of illness,
not illness itself. Just the fact of seeing a doctor in the house,
a doctor who has come because of you, has made your wife
feel towards you a certain . . .

SAMIA: Yes. Yes. As soon as I saw you would need sick leave . . .

ADIL: I don't need sick leave. It's the doctor who made me take
it at the time he made out his report. As for me, I'm in no
need of any leave.

DOCTOR: That's quite so.

SAMIA: In any case, Adil, I was unfair to you.

ADIL: Sometimes.

SAMIA: I admit it.

ADIL: Then you won't go to the bathroom before me?

SAMIA: No, never – I've turned over a new leaf, I promise.

ADIL: You won't tell me to get breakfast?

SAMIA: No, I promise. I promise.

ADIL: You won't impose your will and orders on me?

SAMIA: No, I promise. I promise.

ADIL: And what's the secret of this sudden transformation?

SAMIA: I didn't realize that this behaviour of mine towards you
would have such results.

ADIL: What results?

DOCTOR: She means . . . she means your being angry.

ADIL: But I haven't been angry. I used sometimes to feel
annoyance at your behaviour. I was only too often annoyed
with you, but I've never been angry with you.

DOCTOR: You used to repress it.

ADIL: Repress it?

DOCTOR: Repress it deep within yourself. It's this repression that
leads to . . . that leads to . . .

ADIL: Leads to what?

DOCTOR: Leads to . . . to temperamental upsets.

ADIL: Certainly I feel upset, but only for a while.

SAMIA: But maybe you keep some feeling lurking deep inside you.

ADIL: Because of you? No, not at all.

SAMIA: I almost believed this morning you hated me.

ADIL: Hated you?

SAMIA: Yes, because of the insecticide.

ADIL: Do you call that hate? A mere feeling of slight annoyance at your wish to destroy this cockroach.

SAMIA: I didn't recognize its importance.

ADIL: And do you now honestly recognize its importance?

SAMIA: Of course.

ADIL: I doubt it.

SAMIA: And why do you doubt it?

ADIL: Because you don't watch it with sufficient attention. Look! For example, it has now begun to stand for long periods on the bottom of the bath. What's the meaning of that?

SAMIA (looking with attention): It means that . . .

ADIL: That it's beginning to take rests.

SAMIA: Yes.

ADIL: After that continuous effort it must be in need of rest periods during which it lies prostrate, as you see, quietly moving its whiskers before carrying on anew with its climbing.

DOCTOR (looking with attention): It's actually begun moving slowly so as to start climbing again.

SAMIA: That's right – it's started to climb.

ADIL: Note carefully the spot at which it begins to slip.

SAMIA: Yes, yes – the same spot. There it goes – it's slipped!

DOCTOR: And fallen once more to its place at the bottom.

ADIL: Look, it's getting up from its fall and is beginning to climb again.

SAMIA: And it will slip down again. There it is – it's slipped down! The poor thing! It's been doing exactly the same thing since early morning.

ADIL: And maybe since last night, because when we got up we found it already in the bath. It must therefore have fallen into it from the ceiling during the night.

SAMIA: I have a question, Adil? May I?

ADIL: Of course, Samia – ask it.

SAMIA: Have you not thought of rescuing it from its predicament?

ADIL: Rescuing it?

SAMIA: Yes, why don't you rescue it?

ADIL: It's rescuing itself.

SAMIA: How can it rescue itself? It will never be able to. All the time its attempts are in vain because the bath is empty and slippery; there's nothing for it to climb up but the slippery sides on which it loses its foothold.

ADIL: That's up to it.

SAMIA: At least help it. Give it a little help, Adil. For example, let the end of the towel hang over inside the bath, or bring a piece of string and dangle it over the side – or anything that'll help it to get out.

ADIL: And why should we do that?

SAMIA: To get it out, to get it out alive. Don't you want it to be saved?

ADIL: Who said I wanted it to be saved?

SAMIA: How odd! You don't want it to be saved? Then you want its death?

ADIL: I don't want its death either.

SAMIA: Then what do you want for it?

ADIL: I don't want anything for it. It is no concern of mine.

SAMIA: Of course not. Of course not. It's absolutely no concern of yours. You have no connection with it, no connection at all. You are something and it is something else. We know that only too well, isn't that so, Doctor?

DOCTOR: Without doubt.

SAMIA: Be sure, Adil, that we're *completely* convinced that you have no connection with this cockroach. We wish you to know this well and to believe it.

ADIL: And don't I know this?

SAMIA: The important thing is that you should believe it deep inside you.

ADIL: Believe what?

SAMIA: Believe that there is no relationship and not the slightest similarity between you and it.

ADIL: Similarity between me and it? Whatever next, Samia? Have things come to this pass? You talk of a similarity between me and the cockroach?

SAMIA: On the contrary, it makes me happy to know there's no similarity.

ADIL: Then such a similarity does exist in your view?

SAMIA: Not in mine, Adil.

ADIL: Then in whose?

SAMIA: In your own view?

ADIL: Mine! In my view I resemble the cockroach?

SAMIA: Then you no longer think this is so?

ADIL: Think what? That I resemble the cockroach? In what way do I resemble it? Please let me know. You've really gone too far; this is too much, Samia, much too much. Me resemble a cockroach? Me? In what way? From what point of view? Whiskers? If it's from the point of view of whiskers, I am clean-shaven, as you can see. From the point of view of features? Of lineaments of face? Speak! Speak! Speak!

SAMIA: Please, Doctor, you speak!

DOCTOR (*to Samia*): Be so good as to allow us a moment in private.

SAMIA: I'll go and prepare you a cup of coffee, Doctor. (*She goes out, leaving the doctor and Adil on their own.*)

DOCTOR: Listen, Mr. Adil – you should, first of all, know that your wife is wholly loyal to you and does not at all intend to hurt your feelings.

ADIL: After what I've heard?

DOCTOR: Believe me, she respects you, appreciates you, and has a very high regard for you, despite your belief that your personality is weaker than hers.

ADIL: My personality weaker than hers! Who said so?

DOCTOR: No one at all – a mere supposition, a mere possibility that this was your inner belief.

ADIL: Such a supposition or possibility never occurred to me.

DOCTOR: Maybe, for example, her demands, or what might have been understood as orders, were . . .

ADIL: Certainly she is a person of many demands and orders, even arbitrary actions and a desire to be the boss.

DOCTOR: You admit this point?

ADIL: For sure.

DOCTOR: Then you find that she has a desire to be the boss?

ADIL: Of course, like most wives, and especially those who, like her, have graduated with their husbands from the same college and are employed in the same line of work.

DOCTOR: Equality, then, between the two of you is total in everything?

ADIL: In everything.

DOCTOR: And yet she wants to have the advantage, to be the boss, to dominate.

ADIL: That is exactly my wife's attitude.

DOCTOR: And you let her be the boss and dominate.

ADIL: Yes, and do you know why?

DOCTOR: Because she . . .

ADIL: No, please wait! Don't be too hasty and conclude from

that that she has a stronger personality than me – those are merely her pretensions.

DOCTOR: Her pretensions?

ADIL: Tell me frankly, Doctor, was it not she who said something of that sort to you?

DOCTOR: I believe . . .

ADIL: Yes, I know this of her: deep within her she believes I have a weaker personality than her.

DOCTOR: And is that not true?

ADIL: Of course it's not at all true. She's free to believe whatever she likes about herself. If her conceit portrays things to her in that light, then let her imagine as she will.

DOCTOR: But this does not obviate the fact that you obey her and carry out all her orders.

ADIL: It's a desire on my part to please her, because she's a woman, a weak woman, taken up with her youth, her advancement, her talent. I don't like to shake her belief in her own strength and superiority. I would regard that as meanness, meanness on my part as a strong man. I hold that real manliness demands that she be made to feel her strength and her importance and to raise her morale.

DOCTOR: Raise her morale? Extraordinary! The problem's reversed.

ADIL: What problem?

DOCTOR: Another question, Mr. Adil: the problem of the cockroach?

ADIL: What about the cockroach?

DOCTOR: It's your interest in it?

ADIL: And what's the secret of your interest in my interest?

DOCTOR: None at all, it's just . . .

ADIL: Listen here, Doctor – the whole thing's becoming clear to me. I've now understood. I've understood its beauty and its whiskers and its personality and the similarity. What you were getting at, therefore, was that I . . .

DOCTOR: Frankly, Mr. Adil, sir, yes.

ADIL: Yes?

DOCTOR: Our whole object was merely to assist and to . . .

ADIL: Participate – to assist and participate with my wife in such talk.

DOCTOR: No, Mr. Adil, this is a well-known theory.

ADIL: Theory? What theory?

DOCTOR: To tell you the truth I've not specialized in psychiatry, I've only studied it purely as a hobby, and so . . .

ADIL: Quite understood. And so you came to believe that I belonged to the cockroach species.

DOCTOR: No, it's not quite like that. In any case I've now changed my opinion.

ADIL: Thank God! You now see that I'm a human being!

DOCTOR: You must excuse me, Mr. Adil, but all the surrounding circumstances drew one in that direction.

ADIL: Please, Doctor, explain to me in detail what got into your mind, according to your psychiatry.

DOCTOR: No, there's no point now. I'm sorry.

ADIL: And my wife Samia knew of this opinion of yours?

DOCTOR: Yes.

ADIL: And she it was who helped you to see me as a cockroach?

DOCTOR: No, Mr. Adil, no. It's not like that. It's not, I assure you, quite like that. I assure you.

ADIL: Listen, Doctor, I want to tell you in all frankness that any similarity between me and the cockroach is mere . . .

DOCTOR: My apologies. My apologies, Mr. Adil. Our intentions were well-meant, I swear they were.

ADIL: Allow me to complete what I had to say: if you believed that I resembled a cockroach, then you were mistaken.

DOCTOR: Of course – and how! I admit I made a wrong analysis, that I'm mistaken, a hundred per cent mistaken.

ADIL: Yes, a grave mistake, because I am unable to attain the magnificent level reached by cockroaches.

DOCTOR: What are you saying? The magnificent level?

ADIL: Yes.

DOCTOR: Are you being serious?

ADIL: Wholly serious – and I'm prepared to repeat what I said.

DOCTOR: Then you admire this cockroach?

ADIL: And I appreciate it.

DOCTOR: And you appreciate it?

ADIL: And I respect it.

DOCTOR: And you respect it?

ADIL: And I understand it well.

DOCTOR (*scrutinizing him closely*): Understood. Understood. And you take after it and imagine yourself . . .

ADIL: In its place?

DOCTOR: Yes, like it.

ADIL: Yes, I imagine that.

DOCTOR: Then you, you . . .

ADIL: I what?

DOCTOR: I don't know any longer. You've bewildered me, Mr. Adil.

ADIL: Please, Doctor, that's quite enough. Once again you're applying your psychiatry to me. It's a lot simpler than all that. I shall explain it to you clearly if you'll allow me.

DOCTOR: Please go ahead.

ADIL: First of all, imagine you're a cockroach.

DOCTOR: Me?

ADIL: Or that the cockroach is you.

DOCTOR: Mr. Adil . . .

ADIL: Please don't look at me like that. I understand exactly the meaning of your glances. You are still doubting. You are really at a loss about me, but I assure you once again that it's altogether different from what you have in mind.

DOCTOR: Then your employment of these words is in the nature of a pleasantry or . . .

ADIL: Take it in any meaning you like. The important thing is for you to leave out, as far as I'm concerned, this psychiatric business and be natural with me.

DOCTOR: Be natural?

ADIL: Yes, are you being natural now?

DOCTOR: By God, I'm . . . to tell the truth . . .

ADIL: You're not sure?

DOCTOR: I no longer know anything.

ADIL: I'll tell you what to do: just let yourself go, forget you're a doctor and let's examine the matter with the utmost simplicity. Are you ready to do this?

DOCTOR: Yes.

ADIL: Great! What was I asking you?

DOCTOR: You asked me about . . .

ADIL: Yes, I remember. I asked you to imagine that you . . .

DOCTOR: That I was a cockroach.

ADIL: Or that the cockroach was you.

DOCTOR: Indeed. Indeed.

ADIL: And now to the second step.

DOCTOR: But wait, in my situation I can't . . .

ADIL: Can't what?

DOCTOR: I can't be a cockroach.

ADIL: Why not.

DOCTOR: Because I've never been married.

ADIL: What's that got to do with it?

DOCTOR: It seems that I . . . that I expressed myself badly.

ADIL: No, you merely misunderstood me. I did not ask you to be a family cockroach, in the psychological sense. No, I meant the actual cockroach in front of you there in the bath.

DOCTOR (*pointing at the cockroach in the bath*): That?

ADIL: Yes, that hero.

DOCTOR: Hero?

ADIL: Indeed a hero. Imagine yourself in a deep well with walls of smooth marble and that you found it impossible to get out despite having made exhausting efforts to do so, what would you do?

DOCTOR: I'd give up of course.

ADIL: But it hasn't given up.

DOCTOR: By no means – I see it repeating its attempts dozens of times.

ADIL: Even hundreds. Since early morning I've been occupied in counting up the number of times.

DOCTOR: Is that what you were engaged in since morning?

ADIL: Yes, I wanted to know when its struggle would come to an end.

DOCTOR (*looking into the bath with real interest*): As of now it looks as if it won't give up yet.

ADIL: Indeed. We're tired from watching but it's not tired from trying.

DOCTOR (*continuing to watch it*): What hope has it of escaping?

ADIL: No hope of course.

DOCTOR: Unless you were to intervene and save it.

ADIL: And I shall not intervene.

DOCTOR: Why not, seeing that you admire it?

ADIL: I must leave it to its fate.

DOCTOR: Were it able to scream, and it screamed to you for help, would you not take pity on it?

ADIL: Perhaps, but it's mute and doesn't scream.

DOCTOR: Who are you to say that?

ADIL: What are you saying?

DOCTOR: I am saying that who are we to say it is not screaming now and asking for help – just that the oscillations of its voice are not picked up by the human ear.

ADIL: Very possibly.

DOCTOR: Imagine that it is now screaming and beseeching, and you don't hear and don't understand its language.

ADIL: It also doesn't hear me and see me.

DOCTOR: Yes, every contact between the two of you is severed.

ADIL: Not completely severed, as is borne out by the fact that I am interested in it.

DOCTOR: You are interested in its struggle for life.

ADIL: This, then, is its voice, its pleading, its language which I can hear and understand.

DOCTOR: Certainly, it explains our being so interested in its struggle.

ADIL: Is that not what has kept me in front of the bath since early morning?

DOCTOR (*looking into the bath*): It is in reality an entertaining spectacle.

ADIL (*also looking*): Isn't it.

DOCTOR: Truly, though, I'm surprised at your refraining to help it a little, even by way of remuneration for the spectacle.

ADIL: It really deserves it.

DOCTOR: We're in this together – let's get it out of its plight!

ADIL: Get it out alive?

DOCTOR: Of course.

ADIL: And will Samia accept that?

DOCTOR: She's got a kind heart.

ADIL: I personally prefer not to introduce sentiment into a situation like this, otherwise our position is going to appear truly ridiculous.

Samia appears in the doorway carrying the coffee.

DOCTOR: Quite the contrary, the position now is no longer ridiculous at all. It's become understood and acceptable, and I myself have begun to find the subject worth following.

SAMIA (*offering him the coffee*): Coffee, Doctor.

DOCTOR (*without raising his eyes from the bath*): Thanks, I'll have it in a moment.

SAMIA: It seems that the cockroach is also occupying you, Doctor?

DOCTOR (*continuing his viewing*): Certainly it's begun to interest me.

SAMIA: No doubt the disease is catching!

ADIL (*turning to her*): What disease?

SAMIA: The doctor understands what I mean.

DOCTOR (*rousing himself*): Come along, let's drink the coffee first.

They all go into the bedroom. The doctor sits down in a chair and Samia puts the tray of coffee on a small table beside him.

SAMIA: Have you finished your examination, Doctor?

ADIL: Whose examination? My examination?

SAMIA: No, Adil, I'm just having a word with the doctor.

DOCTOR: I think it's best now to talk openly, for there's no reason or necessity for hiding anything. Mr. Adil is in perfect health and vigour, and can put on his clothes and go out as of now if he wants.

SAMIA: And the sick leave, Doctor?

DOCTOR: That's another question. However, Madam, your husband is in the right about everything and I completely endorse his behaviour, there being nothing at all untoward about it.

SAMIA: And the cockroach?

DOCTOR: What about the cockroach? I myself hope that I could become like the cockroach.

SAMIA (*winking at the doctor*): Ah, understood. I understand, Doctor.

DOCTOR: No, honestly, I'm speaking seriously.

SAMIA: Speaking seriously?

ADIL: Of course, Samia, it's serious. The doctor has explained everything to me, has been absolutely open with me. In any case, may God be indulgent towards you!

SAMIA: Is that right, Doctor?

DOCTOR: The fact is that we had understood the situation wrongly and took up an erroneous attitude.

SAMIA: Meaning that Adil . . .

DOCTOR: Absolutely, a hundred per cent.

SAMIA: Thanks be to God. Thanks be to God. I was extremely worried about you, Adil.

ADIL: You thought there was some sort of kinship between me and the cockroach!

SAMIA: You shouldn't blame me, Adil; your great love for it . . .

DOCTOR: On the contrary, it appears it wasn't love or anything of the sort, because if he'd loved it he'd have had pity on it and saved it. Our whole hope now lies in your compassion.

SAMIA: My compassion?

DOCTOR: Yes – and I personally would ask you, I would intercede with you . . .

SAMIA: Intercede for whom, Doctor?

DOCTOR: For the cockroach.

SAMIA (*shouting*): Doctor! Doctor! Adil, what's happened to the doctor?

DOCTOR: Don't be upset. Don't be upset. I'm fine and well.

SAMIA: Fine and well – like my husband!

ADIL: Yes, like me of course.

SAMIA: What a disaster – you and the doctor! There's only Umm Attiya and I left. It'll be our turn next. No, it can't be – I'm going out at once. Umm Attiya! Umm Attiya!

ADIL: What's happened, Samia? Have you gone mad?

SAMIA: Is it I who've gone mad?

DOCTOR: Calm down, Madam, and allow us to explain things to you.

COOK (*appearing*): You called, Ma'am?

SAMIA: Yes, I'm going out. Prepare my bath.

COOK: Certainly, Ma'am.

She quickly enters the bathroom and turns on the bath tap.

ADIL (*not conscious of what is happening in the bathroom, he walks towards his wife*): Calm down, Samia. Calm down a little and allow us to explain things to you.

DOCTOR: Your nerves are upset, Madam, without proper reason – if you'd only allow us to say a word.

SAMIA: No, there's no point, Doctor.

ADIL: Don't you want to come to an understanding?

SAMIA: It's enough the understanding between you and the doctor – you're both in league against me.

DOCTOR: Not against you, Madam. Would it be reasonable? It's only that I've become convinced by Mr. Adil's point of view; I've understood the true meaning of his purpose and behaviour.

SAMIA: And so you've become like him.

ADIL: Like me? You mean like a cockroach.

DOCTOR: That's an honour for me.

SAMIA: You see, it really is catching!

The cook in the bathroom, having turned on the tap and filled the bath, stretches out her hand and removes the cockroach, dead, with the tip of her fingers, throwing it into a corner of the bathroom.

COOK: I've run the bath, Ma'am!

ADIL (*realizing what has happened*): She's filled the bath! (*He hurries into the bathroom and gives a shout after looking into the bath.*) Come along here, Doctor – what we feared has happened.

DOCTOR (*following him*): What's happened?

ADIL: The cockroach is dead.

DOCTOR: Dead?

ADIL: It was no doubt drowned. But where is it? Umm Attiya, where's the cockroach that was here in the bath?

COOK (*pointing to the corner of the bathroom*): I threw it down there, for the time being. (*She goes out.*)

ADIL: What a pity!

DOCTOR: Yes, it certainly is a pity.

SAMIA: Shall I get you a professional mourner? Shall we bring some music and you can walk in its funeral procession?

ADIL: That's quite enough sarcasm, thank you!

DOCTOR: Let the matter rest, Mr. Adil. What's happened has happened. In any case you wanted to leave it to its fate, and this is its fate.

ADIL: Yes, it had to end – somehow. Let us cast a last look at its corpse.

DOCTOR: Where's its corpse?

SAMIA: Its corpse? Even you, Doctor!

Adil and the doctor look round for the cockroach in the corner of the bathroom.

ADIL: Look. Look, Doctor, at these ants. Where have they come from?

DOCTOR (*looks*): Yes, a horde of ants is carrying it off.

SAMIA: Ants?

ADIL: Yes, ants carrying off the corpse of the cockroach. Come, Samia, look! It's a really extraordinary sight – a crowd of ants carrying off the cockroach and taking it up the wall. Look, Doctor, they're taking it towards one of those cracks.

DOCTOR (*continuing to look*): It's obviously their house, or their village, or their warehouse in which they'll store this booty.

ADIL: Take note of that ant in the front. Do you see it?

DOCTOR: Yes, it's dragging the cockroach by its whiskers.

ADIL: As though it were a ship's tow rope.

DOCTOR: And this group of ants in the rear, they're pushing it from the back. Do you see?

ADIL: The work's distributed amongst them with extraordinary discipline.

DOCTOR: And the most extraordinary thing is that they're going up at speed, despite their heavy load.

ADIL: There's only a short distance left between them and the crack or warehouse. But look, Doctor, it seems as if the opening is too small for the size of the cockroach. How can it be got in?

DOCTOR: Don't be afraid, it'll get in – nothing is too difficult for the genius of ants.

SAMIA (*looking at them from the door*): Having finished with the heroism of cockroaches we've now started on the genius of ants!

ADIL (*continuing to watch*): I doubt if it's possible to get the cockroach into that small crack.

DOCTOR (*also watching*): We'll soon see.

The telephone rings.

SAMIA (*hurrying to the phone*): Telephone, Adil! Perhaps it's for you.

ADIL (*turns and joins her*): For me?

SAMIA (*taking up the receiver*): Hullo. Who did you say? The doctor? Yes, he's here. Just a moment. (*She calls out.*) It's for you, Doctor.

DOCTOR (*hurrying over and taking up the receiver*): Hullo. The company. Yes, I'm the doctor. How do you do? Where's this case? Street . . . number . . . Wait while I write it down. (*Takes out a small notebook and writes.*) What did you say the number was? Thank you. The case I'm on at present? Oh, I've finished with that now. Quite satisfactory. No, not at all serious. Merely indisposed. I'll tell him. Thanks. (*He puts down the receiver.*)

ADIL: They're asking about me at the company?

DOCTOR: Naturally.

SAMIA: They thought it was a serious case.

DOCTOR (*to Adil*): They express their hopes for your recovery.

ADIL: Recovery?

SAMIA: And I too join my voice to theirs.

ADIL: Yes? Yes?

In the meantime the cook has slipped into the bathroom carrying a bucket of water and a rag and has begun cleaning it and removing the ants from off the wall. The others, occupied in their conversation, have not noticed.

DOCTOR (*looking at his watch*): I must leave you – there's another case waiting for me.
SAMIA: Another case?
DOCTOR: In a far-away street. I mustn't be late. Goodbye.
ADIL: Wait, Doctor. Are you going off just like that without taking a look at the ants?
SAMIA: Do you want to hold the doctor up for the ants as well?
DOCTOR: It would in fact interest me, let's go and have a look.
ADIL: Off we go, perhaps the ants will have succeeded in getting the cockroach into that crack.
SAMIA (*looking at them in wonder*): By God, it's amazing!

As Adil and the doctor reach the bathroom the cook leaves it with her bucket.

COOK (*to Samia*): I've cleaned the bathroom, Ma'am.

Samia is busy taking her clothes out of the wardrobe.

ADIL (*in the bathroom*): What a disaster it would be if Umm Attiya's done it.
COOK (*without understanding*): Done it?
ADIL (*shouting as he stands in front of the wall*): What a pity! What a pity!
DOCTOR (*standing behind him and looking at the wall*): She's done it!
ADIL: She's done it. Look – she's removed the ants, the cockroach and the lot. She's cleared the wall of everything.
DOCTOR (*coming out of the bathroom*): Bad luck!
ADIL (*to the cook as he comes out*): Why, Umm Attiya? Why?
COOK: What have I done?
ADIL: Nothing, nothing at all – just carry on with your work, God damn you!

The cook goes out in bewilderment. The doctor takes up his bag.

DOCTOR: I trust you'll spend your day resting and return to work tomorrow feeling a lot better, God willing.
ADIL: And what's keeping me till tomorrow? I'll get dressed now and go to work immediately.

DOCTOR: No, please, you're supposed to be on leave today.

ADIL: And what can I do now with this leave? Can't you cancel it?

DOCTOR: How can I cancel it? The company knows I'm here and that I've come to see you. What shall I say to them? Shall I say that he's . . .

SAMIA: That he's been sitting and watching a cockroach!

DOCTOR: Don't complicate things, Mr. Adil – a day's sick leave and that's that and the problem's solved.

SAMIA (*taking up her clothes*): I'm going into the bathroom. If you'll excuse me. I think it's no longer forbidden to go into the bathroom!

ADIL: Lucky you!

SAMIA: Advise him, Doctor, to spend his day off doing something useful.

ADIL: And what, in your view, is doing something useful?

DOCTOR: Anyway, Mr. Adil knows how to spend his time usefully and enjoyably.

SAMIA: I can bet he'll be spending the day sitting down writing memoirs about the fate of the cockroach!

DOCTOR: And where's the cockroach now? No sign is left of it, not even one of its whiskers.

ADIL: The important thing was its struggle for life.

DOCTOR: Yes, and that is what will remain fixed in my memory. Goodbye, everyone.

SAMIA: We're most grateful, Doctor. We're sorry for having kept you with us all this time without proper reason.

DOCTOR: Not at all. Not at all.

SAMIA: I hope that the case to which you are going is a little more serious!

DOCTOR: You may be sure that I didn't waste my time uselessly with yourselves. Goodbye. (*He leaves hurriedly.*)

SAMIA (*as she enters the bathroom*): Listen, Adil, you've got the day off today. You should know that I want you to spend this day usefully. D'you hear? There are my clothes and dresses all crumpled up in the wardrobe – get down to sorting them out and hang them up at your leisure one by one so that when I come back from work I'll find everything nicely sorted out and organized. Understood?

Adil remains silent, his head lowered.

SAMIA: D'you hear what I say?

ADIL: I do.

SAMIA: And let's not find a single dress creased or crumpled. Understood?

ADIL (*shouting*): Understooooood!

SAMIA: I'm warning you. (*She goes into the bathroom and locks herself in.*)

ADIL (*shouting*): Umm Attiya, bring the bucket and rag and wipe me out of existence!

CURTAIN

The Song of Death

Characters

ASAKIR
MABROUKA
ALWAN, Asakir's son
SUMEIDA, Mabrouka's son

The Song of Death

A peasant house in Upper Egypt. Two women are sitting by the entrance dressed in black: they are Asakir and Mabrouka. A step or two away from them stand a calf and a goat eating grass and dried clover. The two women are sitting in silence with heads lowered. The sound of a train's whistle is heard.

MABROUKA (*raising her head*): That's the train.

ASAKIR (*without moving*): D'you think he's on it?

MABROUKA: Didn't he say so in his letter which Sheikh Mohamed al-Isnawi, the assistant schoolmaster, read over to us yesterday?

ASAKIR: I hope, Mabrouka, you haven't told anyone he's my son.

MABROUKA: Am I crazy? Your son Alwan was drowned in the well at the water-wheel when a child of only two years. The whole village knows that.

ASAKIR: But they still can't quite swallow that story.

MABROUKA: Who are *they* – the Tahawis?

ASAKIR: Didn't your son Sumeida tell you what he heard in the market the other day?

MABROUKA: What did he hear?

ASAKIR: He heard one of them say, in a crowd of people, that either the Azizis have nothing but women left, or they are hiding a man to take vengeance – a man nearer to the murdered man than his cousin Sumeida.

MABROUKA: Yes, my son Sumeida did say that. Were it not for this rumour he wouldn't be able to walk about the village with raised head.

ASAKIR: Let them learn today that the son of the murdered man is still alive. There is no reason to fear for him now that he has attained manhood. It is no longer I who live in fear but those who cannot sleep at night for fear. Bring him quickly, train, quickly, for I have waited so long! Seventeen years! I have counted them up hour by hour. Seventeen years! I have milked them from Time's udders drop by drop just as the milk drips out from the udder of an old cow.

MABROUKA (*listening to the sound of a whistle*): There's the train as it enters the station. He'll find my son Sumeida waiting for him.

ASAKIR (*as though talking to herself*): Yes.

MABROUKA (*turning towards her*): What's wrong, Asakir? You're trembling?

ASAKIR (*as though talking to herself*): Sumeida's song will tell me.

MABROUKA: Tell you?

ASAKIR: About whether he's come.

MABROUKA: You told my son to sing as a sign that Alwan had come?

ASAKIR: Yes, as they approach together from the district office.

MABROUKA: Take heart, Asakir. Take heart. Much has passed, only little yet remains.

ASAKIR: What I feel now is neither fear nor weakness.

MABROUKA: The days of fear have gone never to return. I shall never forget that day I hid your son Alwan when he was two years old in the large basket of meal and carried him off by night, taking him out of the village to Cairo to put him with your relative who worked as a grinder in the perfume shop in the district of Sayyidna al-Hussein.

ASAKIR: I told him: bring him up as a butcher so that he can use a knife well.

MABROUKA: He didn't carry out your wish.

ASAKIR: No, he did – when he was seven years old he put him into a butcher's shop, but the boy ran away.

MABROUKA: To join al-Azhar University.

ASAKIR: Yes, and when I went to see him last year, I found him dressed in his turban and gibba, looking very dignified. I said to him: 'If only your father could have seen you like this he would have been proud of you.' But they didn't allow him to see his son grow up and know such joy.

MABROUKA: Wouldn't it have been better if he'd stayed on at the butcher's shop?

ASAKIR: Why do you say that, Mabrouka?

MABROUKA: I don't know, a passing thought.

ASAKIR: I know that thought.

MABROUKA: What is it, Asakir?

ASAKIR: It hurts you that my son puts a turban and gibba while yours goes on wearing a skullcap and rough peasant gown.

MABROUKA: I swear to you, by the soul of the departed, that such a thing never occurred to me.

ASAKIR: Then why do you hate Alwan being at Al-Azhar University?

MABROUKA: By God, it's not that I hate it, only that I fear . . .

ASAKIR: Fear what?

MABROUKA: That . . . that he does not know well how to use a knife.

ASAKIR: Have trust. Have trust, Mabrouka. When you see Alwan now that he has grown into a man you'll find that he has the strength of arm you know about in the Azizis.

MABROUKA (*listening to the whistle*): The train is leaving the station.

ASAKIR: Let it leave to where it will just so long as it has brought us Alwan to take away the life of the murderer and leave him a rotting corpse for the farm dogs.

MABROUKA: And if he hasn't come?

ASAKIR: Why do you say that, Mabrouka?

MABROUKA: I don't know – just speculation.

ASAKIR: And what would prevent him from coming?

MABROUKA: And what is there to induce him to leave the civilization of Cairo and of Al-Azhar to come here?

ASAKIR: It's his birthplace, it's where blood calls out to him for revenge.

MABROUKA: How far our village is from Cairo! Can the voice of blood reach to the capital?

ASAKIR: Do you believe he won't come?

MABROUKA: I know no better than you, Asakir.

ASAKIR: And his letter which the schoolmaster read for us?

MABROUKA: Have you forgotten that he said in it: 'Perhaps I'll come if circumstances permit.' Who knows whether the circumstances have permitted or not?

ASAKIR: Don't break my spirit, Mabrouka. Don't destroy the hope of someone who heard the train whistles turn to trilling cries of joy in her heart as they made it known that this long period of mourning was nearly at an end. Alwan not coming? What would be my fate? Until when would I have to wait for another time?

MABROUKA: The station is not far away and the district office is close by. If he had come Sumeida would by now have started to sing.

ASAKIR: Perhaps they're walking leisurely and talking together.

It's more than three years ago since they met – the last time
your son went off to Cairo at the time of the birthday feast of
Sayyidna al-Hussein.

MABROUKA: If he'd come my son would be so overjoyed
he'd have burst into song before reaching the district office.

ASAKIR: Perhaps he forgot about it.

MABROUKA: He couldn't forget.

ASAKIR (listening): I don't hear singing.

MABROUKA (listening): Nor I.

ASAKIR: No one singing – not even a shepherd. Nothing singing –
not even an owl in some ruins. I believe, Mabrouka, that he
has not come.

MABROUKA (as though talking to herself): My heart tells me
something.

ASAKIR: My heart, too, my heart that is as sealed as a tomb, as
hard as rock, has now begun to tell me things.

MABROUKA: What does it tell you?

ASAKIR: Of things that will happen.

MABROUKA: Tell me.

ASAKIR (listening hard): Quiet! Listen! Listen! Do you hear,
Mabrouka? Do you hear?

MABROUKA: Sumeida's singing.

ASAKIR: Oh what joy!

*They listen with all their attention to Sumeida's song which is
heard coming from outside more and more clearly.*

SUMEIDA (singing outside in the dialect of Upper Egypt):
> Friend, what excuses have we given,
> What assurances that we'd repent?
> And when your blame you yet continued
> Our shirt and outer robe we rent.
> When of the father I did hear
> My shame no bounds did know,
> And both mine eyes did open wide
> And copious tears did flow.

ASAKIR: Has he come? Has Alwan come? Today I'll rend the
garment of shame and put on the robes of self-respect.

MABROUKA: And we'll hold a funeral for the departed.

ASAKIR: And slaughter the goat and calf for his soul.

MABROUKA: Oh what joy! (She is about to let forth trilling cries of
joy.)

ASAKIR (*stopping her*): Not now, or things will be revealed before their time.

MABROUKA: From now, Oh Suweilam Tahawi, your hours are numbered.

There is a knock at the door. Asakir hurries to open it. Sumeida appears carrying a bag.

SUMEIDA: I've brought Sheikh Alwan.

He puts the bag on the ground and Alwan follows him in.

ASAKIR (*opening her arms to Alwan*): My son, Alwan, my boy!

ALWAN (*kisses his mother on the head*): Mother!

ASAKIR (*to her son*): Give greetings to your aunt Mabrouka!

ALWAN (*turning*): How are you, Aunt Mabrouka?

MABROUKA: Things are unchanged with us, Alwan. Our hopes lie in you.

SUMEIDA: Let us go now to our house, Mother.

MABROUKA: Yes, Asakir, the hour of release is near!

Mabrouka goes off with her son Sumeida. Only Asakir and Alwan remain onstage.

ASAKIR: Aren't you hungry, Alwan? I have a bowl of curds.

ALWAN: I am not hungry, Mother, I ate some bread and eggs on the train.

ASAKIR: Aren't you thirsty?

ALWAN: Nor thirsty.

ASAKIR: No, you have not come for our food or our drink – you have come to eat of his flesh and to drink of his blood.

ALWAN (*like someone in a dream*): I have come, Mother, for something great!

ASAKIR: I know, my son. I know. Wait while I bring you something you have never seen before. (*She hurries off into an inner room.*)

ALWAN (*looking round about him*): My eye still sees in your houses these animals and their droppings, the filth of the water pitcher, and the lengths of firewood and maize stalks roofing over this tumble-down ceiling.

ASAKIR (*appearing from the room carrying a saddlebag which she throws down in front of her son*): Seventeen years I've kept these things for you!

ALWAN (*looks at the saddlebag without moving*): What's this?

ASAKIR: The saddlebag in which your father's body was brought to me, carried upon his donkey. In this pocket I found his head, in the other the rest of his body cut into pieces. They killed him with the knife he was carrying. They put the knife with his body in the saddlebag. Look, this is the knife. I kept it like this with the blood on it so that it's gone rusty. As for the donkey which brought your murdered father, making its way to the house it knew, its head lowered as though mourning its owner, I have been unable to keep it for you: it has died, unable to bear the long years.

ALWAN: And who did all this?

ASAKIR: Suweilam Tahawi.

ALWAN: How did you find out?

ASAKIR: The whole village knows.

ALWAN: Yes, you told me that. You mentioned his name to me dozens of times whenever you came to visit me in Cairo. I was young and unthinking and did not discuss things with you, but today my mind wants to be convinced. What proof is there? Was this crime investigated?

ASAKIR: Investigated?

ALWAN: Yes, what did the district attorney's office say?

ASAKIR: District attorney? For shame! Would we say anything to the district attorney's office? Would the Azizis do such a thing? Did the Tahawis ever do such a thing?

ALWAN: Didn't the district attorney's office question you?

ASAKIR: They asked us and we said we knew nothing and had not seen a body. We buried your father secretly at night.

ALWAN (*as though talking to himself*): So that we might take vengeance into our hands.

ASAKIR: With the same knife with which your father was killed.

ALWAN: And the murderer?

ASAKIR: Alive and well. Alive. There is not a Sheikh's tomb in the district, not a shrine, not a saint at whose grill I have not clung, in whose dust I have not covered my head, at whose grave I have not bared my hair, praying that God might keep him alive till you, my son, bring about his death with your own hand.

ALWAN: Are you sure, Mother, that it is he?

ASAKIR: We have no enemies but the Tahawis.

ALWAN: And how are you to know that it's Suweilam Tahawi himself?

ASAKIR: Because he believes that it was your father who killed his father.

ALWAN: And did my father really kill his father?

ASAKIR: God knows best!

ALWAN: And what's the origin of this enmity between the two families?

ASAKIR: I don't know. No one knows. It's something from of old. All we know is that there has always been blood between them and us.

ALWAN: The origin could be that one day a calf belonging to one of our forefathers drank from a watering-place in a field of one of their forefathers!

ASAKIR: Knowledge about that lies with Him who knows the invisible. All that people know is that between the Azizis and the Tahawis rivers of blood have flowed.

ALWAN: They irrigate no vegetation or fruit.

ASAKIR (*continuing*): They only stopped to flow after the death of your father – because you were so young. The years flowed by, dry like the days of high summer, till people began whispering and others spread false rumours. I twisted and turned on a fire of rage, suppressing my anger, waiting for this moment. And now it has come, so rise up, my son, and quench my fire, water my thirst for revenge with the blood of Suweilam Tahawi!

ALWAN: And has this Suweilam Tahawi a son?

ASAKIR: He has a son of fourteen.

ALWAN: Then I have no more than four or five years left.

ASAKIR: What are you saying?

ALWAN (*continuing*): Until he becomes strong and does to me what I shall do to his father.

ASAKIR: Are you afraid for your life, Alwan?

ALWAN: And you, Mother, are you not afraid for it?

ASAKIR: God is my witness how afraid I am for every hair on your head!

ALWAN: You hold dear my life, Mother?

ASAKIR: And have I any life except through yours, Alwan? Have the Azizis any life except through you? For seventeen years we have all lived only by the breaths you draw.

ALWAN (*with lowered head*): Yes, I understand.

ASAKIR: What feelings of humiliation we have had and how patiently we have suffered harm, yet no sooner does the spectre of you cross our minds than our resolution is spurred

on, our determination is strengthened and we look at each
other in hope, a hope centred on you.

ALWAN (*with head lowered, like someone talking to himself*): Truly you
must have my life.

ASAKIR: Even your father's funeral waits for you, Alwan. These
animals have been prepared for slaughter; my wailing, which
I have imprisoned in my throat all these years, waits for you
to burst forth; my gown that I have refrained from rending
all this time bides your coming; everything in our
existence is lifeless and stagnant and looks to you to charge it
with life.

ALWAN (*as though talking to himself*): Is it thus that you are charged
with life?

ASAKIR: Yes, Alwan. Hasten the promised hour; hasten it, for we
have waited too long.

ALWAN (*in surprise*): The promised hour?

ASAKIR: I have forgotten nothing, not even the stone on which to
sharpen the rusted knife. I have brought it for you and
hidden it in that room.

ALWAN: And how shall I know this Suweilam, never having seen
him in my life?

ASAKIR: Sumeida will lead you to him and will show you where
he is.

ALWAN (*looking at his clothes*): And shall I commit this act dressed
as I am?

ASAKIR: Take off those clothes of yours. I have an *aba* of your
father's, which I have kept for you. (*She moves towards the
inner room.*)

ALWAN (*stopping her*): There's no hurry, Mother. What's the
rush?

ASAKIR: Every breath Suweilam takes with you here is a gift from
you to him.

ALWAN: And what's the harm in that?

ASAKIR: It is taken from our own breaths, is deducted from our
happiness. Despite ourselves we provided him with an
extension of life that has almost put us in our graves. Look
closely at your mother, Alwan! I was in my youth when your
father died. Look at what these years have done to me! It is
as though they were forty years, not seventeen! The sap of
youth has drained away, the bones have lost their vigour, and
no strength is left to me except the unforgettable memory,
the unrelenting heart.

ALWAN (*as though talking to himself*): How heavy is the price of revenge upon the person taking it!

ASAKIR (*not understanding*): What are you saying, Alwan?

ALWAN: I am saying that the Mighty Avenger was merciful to us when He wanted to take from us this burden without paying a price.

ASAKIR (*in a suspicious tone*): What do you mean?

ALWAN: Nothing, Mother. Nothing.

ASAKIR (*in a decisive tone*): Take off your clothes and I'll bring you the *aba*. I'll sharpen the knife with my own hand.

ALWAN: Is there no mosque near-by?

ASAKIR: We have only a small prayer-room near to Sheikh Isnawi's school.

ALWAN (*making a move*): I shall go to it to perform the sunset prayer.

ASAKIR: Now?

ALWAN: I think the sun has almost set.

ASAKIR: Do you want all the people of the village to see you there?

ALWAN: It is the best opportunity for serving my purpose.

ASAKIR (*staring at him*): Are you mad, Alwan?

ALWAN (*continuing*): This meeting with the villagers is for me one of the most important things. Did I not just tell you that I have come for something important?

ASAKIR (*sarcastically*): I can't think you're going to tell the villagers what you've come for!

ALWAN: I must let them all know about it.

ASAKIR: Alwan! My son! What am I hearing from you! Are you being serious? Are you in your right mind? What will you say to them?

ALWAN (*like one in a dream*): I shall tell them what I have come to tell them. For so long I have thought about my village and its people, despite my long absence. In the free time from lessons at al-Azhar, when fellow students gather together, when newspapers are read, and when we are overcome by yearning for the land where we have been raised, we ask ourselves longingly: when will our people in the countryside live like human beings in clean houses where the animals do not eat with them? When will their roofs be covered with something other than twigs from cotton bushes and maize stalks, and their walls be painted with something other than mud and animal dung? When will the water jar be replaced

by clean running water, and electricity take the place of
lanterns? Is that too much to wish for our people? Have not
our people the same rights in life as others?

ASAKIR (*like someone who does not understand*): What talk is this,
Alwan?

ALWAN: This is what the villagers must know, and it is the duty
of us who have been educated in Cairo to open their eyes to
their rights in life. The attainment of this goal is not difficult
for them if they unite and help one another and co-operate
in setting up a council from amongst themselves which will
impose taxes on those who can pay, and to form teams of the
strong and the able who, during their long hours of free time,
will set up bridges and construction works, instead of wasting
it in dissension and squabbles. If they rallied round this idea
and expended serious effort on this task, they could make a
model village here, and it would not be long before all the
villages in the countryside were copying it.

ASAKIR: This bookish talk is something to chat about later on
with Sheikh Mohamed al-Isnawi, who will understand it. As
for now, Alwan, we have more important things before us.

ALWAN (*brought up with a jolt*): What is more important than that?

ASAKIR: Yes, leave off praying tonight in the prayer-room in case
it spoils things. Pray here tonight if you want to. Get up and
take off your clothes and I'll bring you some water from the
jar to wash yourself with, then put on the *aba* and we'll
sharpen the knife together.

ALWAN (*in a whisper with head lowered*): Almighty God, grant me
your mercy, your favour and your pardon.

ASAKIR: What are you saying, Alwan?

ALWAN (*raising his head*): I was saying that I come only to open
people's eyes to life; I bring you life.

ASAKIR: And this is what we have been waiting for patiently for
all these nights – seventeen years with all the Azizis
like the dead, waiting for you to come to bring them back
life!

ALWAN (*in a whisper with head lowered*): Oh God! What shall I do
with these people?

ASAKIR: Why do you keep your head lowered like that? Get up
and don't waste time. Get up.

ALWAN (*taking heart, he raises his head*): Mother, I won't kill!

ASAKIR (*concealing her dismay*): What do I hear?

ALWAN: I won't kill.

ASAKIR (*in a hoarse voice*): Your father's blood!

ALWAN: It is you who have failed him by hiding it from the government – reprisal is for those in power.

ASAKIR (*paying no attention*): The blood of your father!

ALWAN: My hand was not created to bring about someone's death.

ASAKIR (*half out of her mind*): The blood of your father!

ALWAN (*alarmed at her state*): Mother – what's happened to you?

ASAKIR (*as though unconscious of anyone being with her*): The blood of your father . . . seventeen years . . . the blood of your father . . . seventeen years . . .

ALWAN: Calm yourself, Mother. Certainly it is a shock but you must understand that I am not the man to murder with a knife.

ASAKIR (*whispering, like someone possessed*): Seventeen years – revenge for your father – seventeen years.

ALWAN (*as though talking to himself*): I know that you have suffered and endured for a long time, Mother. Were your patience and endurance for a worthwhile end I would have performed miracles for you, but you must understand . . .

ASAKIR (*in a choking voice*): The blood of your father!

ALWAN (*hurrying over to her in alarm*): Mother! Mother! Mother!

ASAKIR (*rousing herself a little in his arms*): Who are you?

ALWAN: Your son Alwan. Your son.

ASAKIR (*coming to her senses and shouting*): My son? My own son? No, never, never!

ALWAN (*taken aback*): Mother!

ASAKIR: I am not your mother. I do not know you. No son issued from my belly.

ALWAN: Try to understand, Mother.

ASAKIR: Get out of my house. God's curse be on you until the Day of Judgement. Get out of my house.

ALWAN: Mother!

ASAKIR (*shouting*): Get out of my house or I shall call the men to put you out. We have our men, there are still men amongst Azizis, but you are not one of them. Get out. Get out of my house.

ALWAN (*taking up his bag*): I shall go to the station to return whence I came. I ask God to calm your agitated soul and shall see you shortly in Cairo; then I shall explain to you my point of view in an atmosphere of calm far away from here. Till we see each other again, Mother!

*He goes off, leaving Asakir in her place, motionless. A moment later
Sumeida appears, putting his head round the door and pushing it open
gently.*

SUMEIDA: Was it you who were shouting, Aunt Asakir?

ASAKIR (*with determination, having recovered her senses*): Come,
  Sumeida!

SUMEIDA (*looking around him*): Where's your son Alwan?

ASAKAI: I have no son, I was not blessed with children.

SUMEIDA: What are you saying, Aunt Asakir?

ASAKIR: Had I a son he would take revenge for his father.

SUMEIDA (*looking round the room*): Where has he gone?

ASAKIR: To the station in order to return to Cairo.

SUMEIDA: My mother was right! When she saw him just now she
  said, as we were going out: 'This gentleman is not the one to
  kill Suweilam Tahawi.'

ASAKIR: Oh that my belly had been ripped apart before bringing
  into the world such a son!

SUMEIDA: Take it easy, Aunt – there are men among the Azizis!

ASAKIR: Our hopes rest in you, Sumeida.

SUMEIDA: A cousin in place of a son.

ASAKIR: But the son is alive. It is he who should avenge the
  blood of his father. He is alive, alive and walking about
  amongst people.

SUMEIDA: Assume that he has died.

ASAKIR: Would that he had actually died as a child in the well
  of the water-wheel. We would not have waited these long
  years, squirming with pain on the coals of suppressed rage,
  waiting futilely. Would that he were dead – we could have
  lived with our excuse and we would not have had to clothe
  ourselves in shame. But he is alive and it has been spread
  abroad in the district, has been circulated in the market
  place that he is alive. What disgrace! What ignominy! What
  shame!

SUMEIDA: Take it easy, Aunt!

ASAKIR: Everything is easy to bear except this disgrace! After it
  life becomes impossible. How can I live in the village when the
  people know that I have such a son? Everyone will spit in
  disgust at the mere mention of his name. From every side
  voices will be raised saying: 'What a failure of a belly that
  brought forth such a child!' Yes, this belly! (*She strikes at her
  belly with violent blows.*) All the women of the village will

scoff at it, even the deformed, the dull-witted, and the barren.
This belly! This belly!

SUMEIDA (*trying to prevent her striking herself*): Aunt Asakir, do not
hurt yourself in this way!

ASAKIR: Bring the knife, Sumeida – I'll rip it open with it!

SUMEIDA: Have you gone mad?

ASAKIR: Sumeida – are you a man?

SUMEIDA (*staring at her*): What do you want?

ASAKIR: Ward off the shame from your cousin!

SUMEIDA: Alwan?

ASAKIR: And from his mother, your Aunt Asakir.

SUMEIDA: What am I to do?

ASAKIR (*taking up the knife from the saddlebag*): Kill him with this
knife!

SUMEIDA: Kill whom?

ASAKIR: Alwan. Plunge this knife into his chest!

SUMEIDA: Kill Alwan? Your son?

ASAKIR: Yes, kill him, bring him to his death.

SUMEIDA: Be sensible, Aunt!

ASAKIR: Do it, Sumeida – for my sake and for his!

SUMEIDA: For his?

ASAKIR: Yes, it is better for him and for me for it to be said that
he was killed than that he shirked taking vengeance for his
father.

SUMEIDA: My cousin!

ASAKIR: If you're a man, Sumeida, don't let him dishonour the
Azizis! After today you will not be able to walk like a man
amongst people; they will whisper about you, will laugh up
their sleeves at you, will point to you in the market places
saying: 'A woman hiding behind a woman!'

SUMEIDA (*as though talking to himself*): A woman?

ASAKIR: If there were such a son amongst the Tahawis, they
would not have allowed him to stay alive for a single hour.

SUMEIDA (*as though talking to himself*): 'A woman hiding behind a
woman!'

ASAKIR: Yes, you – if you accept to condone your cousin after
what has happened!

SUMEIDA (*stretching out his hand resolutely*): Give me the knife!

ASAKIR (*giving him the knife*): Take it – no, wait, I'll wash off the
rust and blood.

SUMEIDA (*impatiently*): Give it here – before he makes his escape
on the evening train.

ASAKIR (*giving him the knife resolutely*): Take it, and may his blood wash off his father's blood that has dried on the blade

SUMEIDA (*leaving with the knife*): If his killing is brought about, Aunt, you will hear my voice raised in song from by the district office.

He goes out hurriedly. Asakir remains alone, rooted to the ground like a statue, her eyes staring out, like someone stupefied. Then Mabrouka appears at the door, carrying a dish on her head.

MABROUKA (*taking the dish from her head*): A salted fish I brought for Sheikh Alwan.

ASAKIR (*turning to her slowly*): Someone has died, Mabrouka!

MABROUKA: God spare you – who?

ASAKIR: Alwan.

MABROUKA: Your son?

ASAKIR: I now have no son, he has become one with the dust.

MABROUKA: What's this you're saying, Asakir? I left him with you just a while ago. Where is he?

ASAKIR: He went to the station to return whence he came and to flee from taking vengeance for his father.

MABROUKA (*with head lowered*): That is what my heart told me.

ASAKIR: Your prediction was right, Mabrouka.

MABROUKA: Would that he had not come!

ASAKIR: Seventeen years we waited!

MABROUKA: And each year you would say, 'He's grown older' – it was as if he were a maize plant that you were measuring each day with the span of your hand, until it had flourished and the corncob had properly ripened; you then tore off the covering only to find that it was empty of seed and fruit.

ASAKIR: If only he had grown up like some useless plant, it would have been easier to bear for we would not have expected to profit from him. As it was, we expected that he would restore our honour. How often, Mabrouka, did I feel proud of him within myself and boast of him in front of you, reckoning that I had produced a son who would wash clean the family honour. And lo! The son I have borne and whom I hid away, as one hides a treasure inside a clay jar, is nothing but a mark of shame that has befallen our tree, just as the blight attacks the cotton bush. A thousand mercies on your soul, O husband of mine whose blood has been spilt! I bore you

the son who will make it possible for your adversaries to
gloat and your enemies to rejoice.

MABROUKA: What degradation for the Azizis!

ASAKIR: Yes, were he to remain alive, but soon he will be buried
in the ground!

MABROUKA (*turning round suddenly*): Where is Sumeida?

ASAKIR (*listening carefully for the sound of a whistle*): Quiet! There's
the evening train entering the station!

MABROUKA: Where's Sumeida, Asakir?

ASAKIR (*listening carefully*): Be quiet! Be quiet! Now at this
moment, at this very moment . . .

MABROUKA (*in surprise*): What about this moment?

ASAKIR (*as though talking to herself*): D'you think he has caught
the train or has he been caught by . . .

MABROUKA: So long as he's gone to the station as you said, he
must have caught the train, and no good will come from all
these pleas for perdition you heap on him.

ASAKIR: Do you really think he's caught the train, Mabrouka?

MABROUKA: And what will stop him?

ASAKIR (*unconsciously*): Sumeida!

MABROUKA: Sumeida? Did he go after him to stop him from
going?

ASAKIR: Yes.

MABROUKA: When did he go?

ASAKIR: Shortly before you came.

MABROUKA: I don't think he'll catch up with him.

ASAKIR (*taking a deep breath*): Do you think so, Mabrouka?

MABROUKA: Unless he ran hard.

ASAKIR (*listening intently for the whistle*): That's the train leaving
the station.

MABROUKA (*staring at her*): What's wrong with you, Asakir?
Why's your face so pale?

ASAKIR: What does your heart tell you, Mabrouka?

MABROUKA: My heart tells me that he's gone.

ASAKIR: Gone, gone – where to?

MABROUKA: Whence he came.

ASAKIR (*staring*): What do you mean?

MABROUKA (*looking at her*): Why are you breathing so heavily,
Asakir?

ASAKIR (*in a whisper, as she glances round distractedly*): Gone to
whence he came?

MABROUKA: Asakir, are you still hoping that some good will
   come out of him?

ASAKIR: No.

MABROUKA: Think of him as never having been.

ASAKIR (*as though talking to herself*): Yes, his death is more of a
   secret than his life.

MABROUKA: Thank God that he is far away.

ASAKIR (*as though asking herself*): Is he now on the train?

MABROUKA: Who knows? Perhaps Sumeida was able to catch up
   with him and to dissuade him from travelling and will
   return with him now.

ASAKIR (*as in a dream*): Return with him now?

MABROUKA: Why not? If Sumeida really went like the wind he'd
   not miss the train.

ASAKIR (*in a whisper*): Will he catch up with him?

MABROUKA: Maybe it won't be long before you see them coming
   along together again.

ASAKIR (*as though talking to herself*): No, this time Sumeida will
   come by himself.

MABROUKA (*looking at her in alarm*): Your face, Asakir, frightens
   me.

ASAKIR (*listening intently*): Quiet! Listen! Listen! Do you now
   hear something?

MABROUKA: No, what should I hear?

ASAKIR: Singing.

MABROUKA (*listening*): No, I don't hear singing.

ASAKIR (*breathing heavily*): Nor I.

MABROUKA: Did Sumeida tell you he'd be singing?

ASAKIR (*in alarm, as though talking to herself*): Perhaps he hasn't yet
   reached the district office.

MABROUKA: I would have thought he had.

ASAKIR (*breathing more heavily*): Reached the district office and
   hasn't sung!

MABROUKA: Why is your face flushed, Asakir?

ASAKIR (*in a whisper*): He hasn't caught up with him.

MABROUKA: You prefer, Asakir, that he does not return, that the
   train carries him far away from this village. I agree with you:
   it is better for him to return to Cairo, to his Sheikhs and his
   colleagues. He does not belong to us now nor we to him. He
   has done well to leave us quickly before he mixes with the
   people of the village and they discover what we have about
   him.

Asakir listens to a far-away sound.

MABROUKA (*turning to her*): You are not listening to me, Asakir. Is not what I'm saying right?

ASAKIR (*in a hoarse, frightening voice*): No, I hear nothing!

MABROUKA (*listening*): But that's Sumeida singing! (*She turns in terror to Asakir.*) Asakir! Asakir! What's happened to you? You're frightening me.

SUMEIDA (*singing from without in the dialect of Upper Egypt*):
> Friend, what excuses have we given,
> What assurances that we'd repent?
> And when your blame you yet continued,
> Our shirt and outer robe we rent.
> When of the father I did hear
> My shame no bounds did know,
> And both mine eyes did open wide
> And copious tears did flow.

ASAKIR (*pulling herself together lest she collapse; even so a faint suppressed cry, like a rattle in the throat, escapes her lips*): My son!

CURTAIN

The Sultan's Dilemma

Characters

THE SULTAN
THE VIZIER
THE CHIEF CADI
A BEAUTIFUL LADY
HER MAIDSERVANT
AN EMINENT SLAVE TRADER
THE CONDEMNED MAN
THE EXECUTIONER
THE WINE MERCHANT
THE MUEZZIN
THE SHOEMAKER
UNKNOWN MAN
1ST LEADING CITIZEN
2ND LEADING CITIZEN
3RD LEADING CITIZEN
1ST MAN IN CROWD
2ND MAN IN CROWD
MOTHER
CHILD
TOWNSPEOPLE
GUARDS
SULTAN'S RETINUE

Act One

An open space in the city during the time of the Mameluke Sultans. On one side there is a mosque with a minaret; on the other, a tavern. In the centre is a house with a balcony. Dawn is about to break and silence reigns. A stake has been set up to which a man, condemned to death, has been tied. His Executioner is nearby trying to fight off sleep.

CONDEMNED MAN (*contemplating the Executioner*): Getting sleepy? Of course you are. Congratulations. Sleep well. You're not awaiting something that will spoil *your* peace of mind.

EXECUTIONER: Quiet!

CONDEMNED MAN: And so – when is it to be?

EXECUTIONER: I told you to be quiet.

CONDEMNED MAN (*pleadingly*): Tell me truly when it's to be? When?

EXECUTIONER: When are you going to stop disturbing me?

CONDEMNED MAN: Sorry. It is, though, something that particularly concerns me. When does this event – a joyous one for you – take place?

EXECUTIONER: At dawn. I've told you this more than ten times. At dawn I'll carry out the sentence on you. Now do you understand? So let me enjoy a moment's peace.

CONDEMNED MAN: Dawn? It's still far off, isn't it, Executioner?

EXECUTIONER: I don't know.

CONDEMNED MAN: You don't know?

EXECUTIONER: It's the Muezzin who knows. When he goes up to the minaret of this mosque and gives the call to the dawn prayer, I'll raise my sword and swipe off your head – those are the orders. Happy now?

CONDEMNED MAN: Without a trial? I haven't yet been put on trial, I haven't yet appeared before a judge.

EXECUTIONER: That's nothing to do with me.

CONDEMNED MAN: For sure, you have nothing to do with anything except my execution.

EXECUTIONER: At dawn, in furtherance of the Sultan's orders.

CONDEMNED MAN: For what crime?

EXECUTIONER: That's not my affair.

CONDEMNED MAN: Because I said . . .

EXECUTIONER: Quiet! Quiet! Shut your mouth – I have been ordered to cut off your head right away if you utter a word about your crime.

CONDEMNED MAN: Don't be upset, I'll shut my mouth.

EXECUTIONER: You've done well to shut your mouth and leave me to enjoy my sleep. It's in your interest that I should enjoy a quiet and peaceful sleep.

CONDEMNED MAN: In my interest?

EXECUTIONER: Certainly, it's in your interest that I should be completely rested and in excellent health, both in body and mind; because when I'm tired, depressed, and strung up, my hand shakes, and when it shakes I perform my work badly.

CONDEMNED MAN: And what's your work to me?

EXECUTIONER: Fool! My work has to do with your neck. Poor performance means your neck will not be cleanly cut, because a clean cut requires a steady hand and calm mind so that the head may fly off at a single blow, allowing you no time to feel any sensation of pain. Do you understand now?

CONDEMNED MAN: Of course, that's quite right.

EXECUTIONER: You see! Now you must be quite convinced why it is necessary that you should let me rest; also, to bring joy to my heart and raise my morale.

CONDEMNED MAN: Your morale? *Yours?*

EXECUTIONER: Naturally, if I were in your shoes . . .

CONDEMNED MAN: O God, take him at his word! I wish you *were* in my shoes.

EXECUTIONER: What are you saying?

CONDEMNED MAN: Carry on. What would you do if you had the honour and good fortune to be in my shoes?

EXECUTIONER: I'll tell you what I'd do – have you any money?

CONDEMNED MAN: Ah, money! Yes, yes, yes! Money! An apposite thought. As for money, my friend, you may say what you like about that. The whole city knows – and you among them – that I'm one of the very richest of merchants and slave-traders.

EXECUTIONER: No, you have misunderstood me – I'm not talking of a bribe. It's impossible to bribe me – not because of my honesty and integrity, but because, quite frankly, I am unable to save you. All I wanted was to accept your invitation to have a drink – if you should happen to do so. A glass of wine is not a bribe. It would be impolite of me to refuse your invitation. Look! There's a Wine Merchant a stone's throw away from you – his tavern is open all night, because he has customers who visit that whore who lives in the house opposite.

CONDEMNED MAN: A drink? Is that all?

EXECUTIONER: That's all.

CONDEMNED MAN: I've got a better and more attractive idea. Let's go up together, you and I, to that beautiful woman. I know her and if we went to her we'd spend the most marvellous night of our lives – a night to fill your heart with joy and gaiety and raise your morale. What do you say?

EXECUTIONER: No, gracious sir.

CONDEMNED MAN: You would accept my invitation to a drink, but refuse my invitation to a party of drinking and fun, beauty and merriment?

EXECUTIONER: In that house? No, my dear condemned friend, I prefer for you to stay as you are: fettered with chains till dawn.

CONDEMNED MAN: What a pity you don't trust me! What if I were to promise you that before the call to dawn prayers I would be back again in chains?

EXECUTIONER: Does a bird return to the snare?

CONDEMNED MAN: Yes, I swear to you on my honour.

EXECUTIONER: *Your* honour? What an oath!

CONDEMNED MAN: You don't believe me.

EXECUTIONER: I believe you so long as you are where you are – and in handcuffs.

CONDEMNED MAN: How can I invite you to have a drink then?

EXECUTIONER: That's easy. I'll go to the tavern and ask him to bring two glasses of his best wine and when he brings them we'll drink them right here. What do you say?

CONDEMNED MAN: But . . .

EXECUTIONER: We're agreed. I'll go – there's no need for you to trouble yourself. Just a minute, with your permission.

The Executioner goes to the tavern at the corner of the square and knocks at the door. The Wine Merchant comes out to him, he whispers something in his ear, and returns to his place.

EXECUTIONER (*to the condemned man*): Everything necessary has been arranged, and you will see, my dear condemned man, the good result shortly.

CONDEMNED MAN: What good result?

EXECUTIONER: My masterful work. When I drink I'm very precise in my work, but, if I haven't drunk, my work goes all to hell. By way of example I'll tell you what happened the other day. I was charged with the job of executing someone, and I hadn't drunk a thing all that day. Do you know what I did? I gave that poor fellow's neck such a blow that his head flew off into the air and landed far away – not in this basket of mine, but in another basket over there, the basket belonging to the Shoemaker next door to the tavern. God alone knows the trouble we had getting the missing head out of the heaps of shoes and soles.

CONDEMNED MAN: The Shoemaker's basket! What a shameful thing to happen! I beseech you by God not to let my head suffer such a fate.

EXECUTIONER: Don't be afraid. Things are different where you are concerned. The other head belonged to a horribly stingy fellow.

The Wine Merchant appears from his shop carrying two glasses.

WINE MERCHANT (*moving towards the condemned man*): This is of course for you – your last wish.

CONDEMNED MAN: No, for the Executioner – it's his cherished wish.

EXECUTIONER (*to the Wine Merchant*): To bring calm and contentment to my heart.

WINE MERCHANT: And from whom shall I receive payment?

CONDEMNED MAN: From me of course – to bring joy and gladness to his heart.

EXECUTIONER: It is incumbent upon me to accept his warm invitation.

CONDEMNED MAN: And it is incumbent upon me to raise his morale.

WINE MERCHANT: What very good friends you two are!

EXECUTIONER: It is a reciprocated affection.

CONDEMNED MAN: Until dawn breaks.

EXECUTIONER: Don't worry about the dawn now – it is still far off. Come, let's touch glasses.

The Executioner snatches up the two glasses and strikes one against the other, turns, raises a glass, and drinks to the condemned man.

EXECUTIONER: Your health!

CONDEMNED MAN: Thank you.

EXECUTIONER (*after he has drained his glass he holds the other glass up to the condemned man's mouth*): And now it's your turn, my dear fellow.

CONDEMNED MAN (*taking a gulp and coughing*): Enough. You drink the rest for me.

EXECUTIONER: Is that your wish?

CONDEMNED MAN: The last!

EXECUTIONER (*raising the second glass*): Then I raise my glass to . . .

CONDEMNED MAN: Your masterful work.

EXECUTIONER: God willing! Also to your generosity and kindness, my friend.

WINE MERCHANT (*taking the two empty glasses from the Executioner*): What's this old slave-trader done? What's his crime? All of us in the city know him – he's no murderer or thief.

CONDEMNED MAN: And yet my head will fall at dawn, just like that of any murderer or thief.

WINE MERCHANT: Why? For what crime?

CONDEMNED MAN: For no reason except that I said . . .

EXECUTIONER: Quiet! Don't utter a word! Shut your mouth!

CONDEMNED MAN: I've shut my mouth.

EXECUTIONER: And you, Wine Merchant, you've got your glasses, so off with you!

WINE MERCHANT: And my money?

EXECUTIONER: It's he who invited me – and only a dastardly fellow refuses an invitation.

CONDEMNED MAN: To be sure I invited him, and he was good enough to accept my invitation. Your money, Tavern Owner, is here in a purse in my belt. Approach and take what you want.

EXECUTIONER: Allow me to approach on his behalf.

He approaches and takes some money from the condemned man's purse and pays the wine merchant.

EXECUTIONER: Take what you're owed and a bit more that you may know we're generous people.

The Wine Merchant takes his money and returns to his shop. The Executioner begins humming in a low voice.

CONDEMNED MAN (*anxiously*): And now . . .

EXECUTIONER: Now we begin our singing and merrymaking. Do you know, my dear condemned man, that I'm very fond of good singing, a pleasant tune, and fine lyrics? It fills the heart with contentment and joy, with gladness and a delight in life. Sing me something!

CONDEMNED MAN: I? Sing?

EXECUTIONER: Yes. Why not? What's to stop you? Your larynx – thanks be to God – is perfectly free. All you have to do is raise your voice in song and out will come a lovely tune to delight the ear. Come on, sing! Entertain me!

CONDEMNED MAN: God bless us! O God, bear witness!

EXECUTIONER: Come along! Sing to me!

CONDEMNED MAN: Do you really think I'm in the mood for singing at this time?

EXECUTIONER: Did you not just now promise me to bring gladness to my soul and remove the depression from my heart?

CONDEMNED MAN: Are you the one to feel depressed?

EXECUTIONER: Yes, please remove my depression. Overwhelm me with joy! Let me enjoy the strains of ballads and songs! Drown me with melodies and sweet tunes! Listen – I've remembered something. I know by heart a song I composed myself during one night of sleeplessness and woe.

CONDEMNED MAN: Then sing it to me.

EXECUTIONER: I don't have a beautiful voice.

CONDEMNED MAN: And who told you that *my* voice was beautiful?

EXECUTIONER: To me all other people's voices are beautiful – because I don't listen to them, especially if I'm drunk. All I'm concerned with is being surrounded on all sides by singing: the feeling that there is singing all around me soothes my nerves. Sometimes I feel as though I myself would like to sing, but one condition must obtain: that I find someone to listen to me. And if there is someone to listen, let him beware if he does not show admiration and appreciation, for if not . . . if not I become shy and embarrassed and begin to tremble, after which I get very angry. Now, having drawn your attention to the condition, shall I sing?

CONDEMNED MAN: Sing!

EXECUTIONER: And will you admire me and show your appreciation?

CONDEMNED MAN: Yes.

EXECUTIONER: You promise faithfully?

CONDEMNED MAN: Faithfully.

EXECUTIONER: Then I'll sing you my tender song. Are you listening?

CONDEMNED MAN: I'm listening and appreciating.

EXECUTIONER: The appreciation comes at the end. As for now, all you're asked to do is merely to listen.

CONDEMNED MAN: I'm merely listening.

EXECUTIONER: Good. Are you ready?

CONDEMNED MAN: Why? Isn't it you who're going to sing?

EXECUTIONER: Yes, but it's necessary for you to be ready to listen.

CONDEMNED MAN: And am I capable of doing anything else? You have left my ears free – no doubt for that purpose.

EXECUTIONER: Then let's start. This tender song, called *The Flower and the Gardener*, was composed by me. Yes, I composed it myself.

CONDEMNED MAN: I know that.

EXECUTIONER: How odd! Who told you?

CONDEMNED MAN: You told me so yourself just a moment ago.

EXECUTIONER: Really? Really? And now, do you want me to begin?

CONDEMNED MAN: Go ahead.

EXECUTIONER: I'm just about to begin. Listen – but you're not listening.

CONDEMNED MAN: I am listening.

EXECUTIONER: The listening must be done with superlative attention.

CONDEMNED MAN: With superlative attention!

EXECUTIONER: Be careful not to upset me by letting your mind wander and not paying attention.

CONDEMNED MAN: I am paying attention.

EXECUTIONER: Are you ready?

CONDEMNED MAN: Yes.

EXECUTIONER: I don't find you excessively enthusiastic.

CONDEMNED MAN: And how should I behave?

EXECUTIONER: I want you to be burning with enthusiasm. Tell me you absolutely insist that you listen to my singing.

CONDEMNED MAN: I absolutely insist . . .

EXECUTIONER: You say it coldly, with indifference.

CONDEMNED MAN: Coldly?

EXECUTIONER: Yes. I want the insistence to issue forth from the depths of your heart.

CONDEMNED MAN: It comes from the depths of my heart.

EXECUTIONER: I don't sense the warmth of sincerity in your voice.

CONDEMNED MAN: Sincerity?

EXECUTIONER: Yes, it's not apparent from the tone of your voice; it is the tone and timbre of the voice that reveals a person's true feelings, and your voice is cold and indifferent.

CONDEMNED MAN: And so – are you going to sing or aren't you?

EXECUTIONER: I shan't sing.

CONDEMNED MAN: Thanks be to God!

EXECUTIONER: You thank God for my not singing?

CONDEMNED MAN: No, I shall always thank God for your singing and your not singing alike. I don't believe there's anyone who'd object to praising God in all circumstances.

EXECUTIONER: Deep down you're wishing that I won't sing.

CONDEMNED MAN: Deep down? Who but God knows a man's inner thoughts?

EXECUTIONER: Then you want me to sing?

CONDEMNED MAN: If you like.

EXECUTIONER: I'll sing.

CONDEMNED MAN: Sing!

EXECUTIONER: No, I have a condition: implore me first of all to sing. Plead with me.

CONDEMNED MAN: I plead with you.

EXECUTIONER: Say it sensitively, entreatingly.

CONDEMNED MAN: Please – I implore you – by your Lord, by the Lord of all creation. I ask of God, the One, the Conqueror, the Strong and Mighty, to soften your cruel heart and to listen to my request and to be so good and gracious as to sing.

EXECUTIONER: Again!

CONDEMNED MAN: What?

EXECUTIONER: Repeat this pleading!

CONDEMNED MAN: God Almighty! Have mercy upon me! You've killed me with all this resistance and coyness. Sing if you want to; if not, then, for God's sake let me be and I'll have nothing to do with it.

EXECUTIONER: Are you angry? I don't want you to be angry. I'll sing so as to calm you down and remove your feeling of distress. I'll start right away. (*He coughs, then hums softly preparatory to singing.*)

CONDEMNED MAN: At last!

EXECUTIONER (*standing up suddenly*): If you'd prefer me not to sing, say so frankly.

CONDEMNED MAN: Heavens above! He's going to start all over again.

EXECUTIONER: Is your patience exhausted?

CONDEMNED MAN: And how!

EXECUTIONER: Am I making you suffer?

CONDEMNED MAN: And how!

EXECUTIONER: Just be patient, my dear fellow. Be patient.

CONDEMNED MAN: This Executioner is really killing me!

EXECUTIONER: What are you saying?

CONDEMNED MAN: I can't stand any more.

EXECUTIONER: You can't stand the waiting. What a poor, pining creature you are, so consumed with wanting to hear my singing! I'll begin then. I shan't make you wait any longer. I'll start right away. Listen! Here's my tender song.

He clears his throat, hums, and then sings in a drunken voice:

> *O flower whose life is but a night,*
> *Greetings from your admirers!*
> *Plucked at dawn of day tomorrow,*
> *The robe of dew from you will fall.*
> *In a firewood basket you will lie*
> *And all around my tunes will die.*
> *In the air the deadly blade will flash*
> *Shining bright in gardener's hand.*
> *O flower, whose life is but a night!*
> *On you be peace, on you be peace!*

Silence.

EXECUTIONER: Why are you silent? Didn't you like it? This is the time to show admiration and appreciation.

CONDEMNED MAN: Is this your tender song, you ill-omened Executioner?

EXECUTIONER: Please – I'm no Executioner.

CONDEMNED MAN: What do you think you are then?
EXECUTIONER: I'm a gardener.
CONDEMNED MAN: A gardener?
EXECUTIONER: Yes, a gardener. Do you understand? A gardener.
I'm a gar - den - er.

A window is opened in the beautiful lady's house, and the maid looks out.

MAID: What's all this now? What's this uproar when people are asleep? My mistress has a headache and wishes to sleep undisturbed.
EXECUTIONER (*sarcastically*): Your mistress! (*He laughs derisively.*) Her mistress!
MAID: I told you to stop that noise.
EXECUTIONER: Take yourself off, server of vice and obscenity.
MAID: Don't insult my mistress! If she wanted to she could have twenty sweepers like you to sweep the dust from under her shoes.
EXECUTIONER: Hold your tongue and take yourself off, you filthiest of creatures!

The lady appears at the window behind her servant.

LADY: What's happening?
MAID: This drunken executioner is raising a din and hurling abuse at us.
LADY: How dare he!
EXECUTIONER (*pointing at the window*): That's her, in all her splendour – her famous mistress!
LADY: Show a little respect, man!
EXECUTIONER (*laughing sarcastically*): Respect!
LADY: Yes, and don't force me to teach you how to respect ladies.
EXECUTIONER: Ladies? (*He laughs.*) Ladies! She says ladies! Listen and marvel!
LADY (*to her maid*): Go down and give him a lesson in manners.
MAID (*to the Executioner*): Wait for me – if you're a man!

The two women disappear from the window.

EXECUTIONER (*to the condemned man*): What does this . . . this she-devil intend to do? Do you know? She's capable of anything. Good God, did you see how she threatened me?

MAID (*emerging from the door of the house, a shoe held high in her hand*): Come here!

EXECUTIONER: What are you going to do with that shoe?

MAID: This shoe is the oldest and filthiest thing I could find in the house – do you understand? I came across nothing older or filthier befitting that dirty, ugly face of yours.

EXECUTIONER: Now the effect of the glass of lovely wine has really flown from my head. Did you hear the nice polite things she was saying, oh condemned man?

CONDEMNED MAN: Yes.

EXECUTIONER: And you utter not a word?

CONDEMNED MAN: I?

EXECUTIONER: And you remain unmoved?

CONDEMNED MAN: How?

EXECUTIONER: You let her insult me like this and remain silent?

CONDEMNED MAN: And what do you want me to do?

EXECUTIONER: Do something! At least say something!

CONDEMNED MAN: What's it got to do with me?

EXECUTIONER: What lack of gallantry, what flagging resolution! You see her raising the shoe in her hand like someone brandishing a sword and you don't make a move to defend me. You just stand there with shackled hands. You just look on without caring. You listen without concern to my being insulted, humiliated, and abused? By God, this is no way to show chivalry.

CONDEMNED MAN: Truly!

MAID (*shaking the shoe in her hand*): Listen here, man! Leave this poor fellow alone. You face up to me if you've got any courage. Your reckoning is with me. You've behaved very rudely towards us and it's up to you to apologize and ask our forgiveness. Otherwise, by the Lord of Hosts, by the Almighty, by the Omnipotent . . .

EXECUTIONER (*gently*): Steady! Steady!

MAID: Speak! What's your answer?

EXECUTIONER: Let's come to an understanding.

MAID: First, ask for forgiveness.

EXECUTIONER: From whom should I ask forgiveness? From you?

MAID: From my mistress.

EXECUTIONER: Where is she?

LADY (*appearing on the threshold of her house*): Here I am. Has he apologized?

MAID: He will do so, milady.

EXECUTIONER: Yes, milady.

LADY: Good. Then I accept your apology.

EXECUTIONER: Only, milady – would it not be best for the waters to flow back to their usual channels and for things to be as before?

LADY: They are.

EXECUTIONER: I meant for the wine to flow back into the channels of my head.

LADY: What do you mean?

EXECUTIONER: I mean that there is a certain damage that requires repairing. Your efficient servant has removed the intoxication from my head. From where shall I fill the void?

LADY: I shall take upon myself the filling of your head. Take as much drink as you wish from the Wine Merchant at my expense.

EXECUTIONER: Thank you, O bountiful lady. (*The Executioner signals to the Wine Merchant who is standing by the door of his tavern to bring him a glass.*)

CONDEMNED MAN (*to the lady*): Do you not know me, beautiful lady?

LADY: Of course I know you. From the first instant when they brought you here at nightfall. I caught sight of you from my window and recognized you and it saddened me to see you in shackles, but – but what crime have you committed?

CONDEMNED MAN: Nothing much. All that happened was that I said . . .

EXECUTIONER (*shouting*): Careful! Careful! Shut your mouth!

CONDEMNED MAN: I've shut my mouth.

LADY: Naturally they gave you a trial?

CONDEMNED MAN: No.

LADY: What are you saying? Weren't you given a trial?

CONDEMNED MAN: I wasn't taken to court. I sent a complaint to the Sultan asking that I be given the right to appear before the Chief Cadi, the most just of those who judge by conscience, the most scrupulous adherent to the canonical law, and the most loyal defender of the sanctity of the law. But – here dawn approaches and the Executioner has had his orders to cut off my head when the call to dawn prayers is given.

LADY (*looking up at the sky*): The dawn? The dawn's almost breaking. Look at the sky!

EXECUTIONER (*in his hand a glass taken from the Wine Merchant*): It's not the sky, my dear lady, that will decide the moment of fate for this condemned man but the minaret of this mosque. I am waiting for the Muezzin.

LADY: The Muezzin. He is surely on his way. Sometimes I stay awake in the morning and I see him at this very moment making for the mosque.

CONDEMNED MAN: Then my hour has come.

LADY: No – not so long as your complaint has not been examined.

CONDEMNED MAN: This Executioner will not await the result of the complaint. Isn't that so, Executioner?

EXECUTIONER: I shall await only the Muezzin. Those are my orders.

LADY: Whose orders? The Sultan's?

EXECUTIONER: Roughly.

CONDEMNED MAN (*shouting*): Roughly? Is it not then the Sultan?

EXECUTIONER: The Vizier – the orders of the Vizier are the orders of the Sultan.

CONDEMNED MAN: Then I am irretrievably lost.

EXECUTIONER: Just so. No sooner does the Muezzin's call to prayer rise up to the sky than your soul rises with it. This causes me great sadness and distress but work is work. A job's a job.

LADY (*turning towards the street*): Oh disaster! Here is the Muezzin – he has arrived.

CONDEMNED MAN: The die is cast.

The Muezzin makes his appearance.

EXECUTIONER: Hurry, O Muezzin – we're waiting for you.

MUEZZIN: Waiting for me? Why?

EXECUTIONER: To give the call to the dawn prayer.

MUEZZIN: Do you want to pray?

EXECUTIONER: I want to carry out my work.

MUEZZIN: What have I to do with your work?

EXECUTIONER: When your voice rises up to the sky the soul of this man will rise with it.

MUEZZIN: God forbid!

EXECUTIONER: Those are the orders.

MUEZZIN: The life of this man hangs on my vocal chords?

EXECUTIONER: Yes.

MUEZZIN: There is no power and no strength save in God!

EXECUTIONER: O Muezzin, hasten to your work so that I may do mine.

LADY: And what's the hurry, kind Executioner? The Muezzin's voice has been affected by the night cold and he is in need of a hot drink. Come into my house, Muezzin. I shall prepare you something which will put your voice to rights.

EXECUTIONER: And the dawn?

LADY: The dawn is in no danger and the Muezzin knows best as to its time.

EXECUTIONER: And my work?

LADY: Your work is in no danger – so long as the Muezzin has not yet called for the dawn prayers.

EXECUTIONER: Do you agree, oh Muezzin?

LADY: He agrees to accepting my little invitation for a short while, for he is among my best friends in the quarter.

EXECUTIONER: And those who have gone to pray in the mosque?

MUEZZIN: There are only two men there. One of them is a stranger to this city and has taken up his abode in the mosque, whilst the other is a beggar who has sought shelter in it from the night cold. All are now deep in sleep and seldom do people pay attention to the call to dawn prayers. Only those get up whom I wake with a kick so that they may perform their religious duties.

LADY: Most of the people of the quarter live a life of ease and sleep well on into the forenoon.

EXECUTIONER: Are you both meaning to say that the call to dawn prayers won't be given today?

LADY: What we mean is ... there's no hurry. There is safety in proceeding slowly, remorse in proceeding hastily. Don't worry yourself! The call to the dawn prayer will be given in good time, and in any event you are all right and are not answerable. The Muezzin alone is responsible. Let us go then, oh Muezzin! A cup of coffee will restore your voice.

MUEZZIN: There's no harm in just a little time and just a small cup.

The lady enters her house with the Muezzin.

EXECUTIONER (*to the condemned man*): Did you see? Instead of going up into the minaret he went up to the house of the . . . the honoured lady. There's the Muezzin for you!

CONDEMNED MAN: A gallant man! He risks everything. As for you, you against whom no censure or blame will be directed, you who are safely covered by your excuse, who bear no liability, possessed as you are of a pretext, it's you who's raging and storming and becoming alarmed. Calm down a little, my friend! Be forbearing and patient! Put your trust in God! Listen, I've got an idea – an excellent, a brilliant idea. It will calm your nerves and bring joy to your soul. Sing me your tender song once again with that sweet, melodious voice of yours, and I swear to you I'll listen to it with a heart palpitating with enthusiasm and admiration. Come along – sing! I'm listening to you with my very being.

EXECUTIONER: I no longer have any desire to.

CONDEMNED MAN: Why? What's upset you? Is it because you didn't lop off my head?

EXECUTIONER: It's because I failed to carry out my duty.

CONDEMNED MAN: Your duty is to carry out the sentence at the time of the call to the dawn prayer. Yet who gives the call to the dawn prayer? You or the Muezzin?

EXECUTIONER: The Muezzin.

CONDEMNED MAN: And has he done so?

EXECUTIONER: No.

CONDEMNED MAN: Then what fault is it of yours?

EXECUTIONER: Truly it is not my fault.

CONDEMNED MAN: This is what we're all saying.

EXECUTIONER: You're comforting me and making light of things for me.

CONDEMNED MAN: I'm telling the truth.

EXECUTIONER (*looking up and down the street and shouting*): What are these crowds? Good God! It's the Vizier's retinue! It's the Vizier!

CONDEMNED MAN: Don't tremble like that! Calm yourself!

EXECUTIONER: It won't be held against me . . . I'm covered, aren't I?

CONDEMNED MAN: Set your mind at rest! You are covered with a thousand blankets of arguments and excuses.

EXECUTIONER: It's the accursed Muezzin who will pay the harsh reckoning.

The Vizier appears surrounded by his guards.

VIZIER (*shouting*): How strange! Has this criminal not been executed yet?

EXECUTIONER: We are awaiting the dawn prayer, milord Vizier, in accordance with your orders.

VIZIER: The dawn prayer? We have performed it at the palace mosque in the presence of Our Majesty the Sultan and the Chief Cadi.

EXECUTIONER: It's not my fault, milord Vizier. The Muezzin of this mosque has not yet gone up to the minaret.

VIZIER: How's that? This is unbelievable. Where is this Muezzin?

The Muezzin comes out drunk from the door of the house and tries to hide himself behind the lady and her maid.

EXECUTIONER (*catching sight of him and shouting*): That's him! There he is!

VIZIER (*to the guards*): Bring him here! (*They bring him before the Vizier.*) Are you the Muezzin of this mosque?

MUEZZIN: Yes, milord Vizier.

VIZIER: Why have you not yet given the call to the dawn prayer?

MUEZZIN: Who told you that, milord Vizier? I gave the call to the dawn prayer some time ago . . .

VIZIER: To the dawn prayer?

MUEZZIN: At its due time, just like every day, and there are those who heard me.

LADY: Truly we all heard him give the call to the dawn prayer from up in the minaret.

MAID: Yes, today as is his habit every day at the same time.

VIZIER: But this Executioner claims . . .

LADY: This Executioner was drunk and fast asleep.

MAID: And the sound of his snoring rose up to us and woke us from our sweet slumbers.

VIZIER (*in astonishment to the Executioner*): Is it thus that you carry out my orders?

EXECUTIONER: I swear, I swear, milord Vizier . . .

VIZIER: Enough of that!

The Executioner is tongue-tied with bewilderment.

CONDEMNED MAN: O Vizier, I would beg you to listen to me. I sent to His Majesty the Sultan a complaint . . .

EXECUTIONER (*collecting his wits and shouting*): I swear, milord Vizier, that I was awake . . .

VIZIER: I told you to keep quiet. (*He turns to the condemned man.*) Yes, your complaint is known to His Majesty the Sultan and he ordered that you be turned over to the Chief Cadi. His Majesty the Sultan will himself attend your trial. This is his noble wish and his irrefutable command. Guards! Clear the square of people and let everyone go home. This trial must take place in complete secrecy.

The guards clear the square of people.

EXECUTIONER: Milord Vizier . . . (*He tries to explain matters but the Vizier dismisses him with a gesture.*)

The Sultan appears with his retinue, accompanied by the Chief Cadi.

CONDEMNED MAN (*shouting*): Your Majesty! Justice! I beg for justice!

SULTAN: Is this the accused?

CONDEMNED MAN: Your Majesty! I have committed no fault or crime!

SULTAN: We shall see.

CONDEMNED MAN: And I haven't been tried yet! I haven't been tried!

SULTAN: You shall be given a fair trial in accordance with your wish, and the Chief Cadi shall be in charge of your trial in our presence. (*The Sultan makes a sign to the Chief Cadi to start the trial, then sits down in a chair which has been brought for him, while the Vizier stands by his side.*)

CADI (*sitting on his chair*): Remove the accused's chains. (*One of the guards undoes the condemned man's fetters.*) Approach, man! What is your crime?

CONDEMNED MAN: I have committed no crime.

CADI: What is the charge brought against you?

CONDEMNED MAN: Ask the Vizier that!

CADI: I am asking *you*.

CONDEMNED MAN: I did nothing at all except utter an innocent word in which there is neither danger nor harm.

VIZIER: It's a terrible and sinful word.

CADI (*to the condemned man*): What is this word?

CONDEMNED MAN: I don't like to repeat it.

VIZIER: Now you don't like to, but in the middle of the market place and amongst throngs of people . . .

CADI: What is this word?

VIZIER: He said that His Majesty, the great and noble Sultan, is a mere slave.

CONDEMNED MAN: Everyone knows this – it is common knowledge.

VIZIER: Don't interrupt me – and he claimed that he was the slave trader who undertook the sale of our Sultan in his youth to the former Sultan.

CONDEMNED MAN: That's true. I swear it by a sacred oath – and it is a matter of pride to me which I shall treasure for all time.

SULTAN (*to the condemned man*): You? You sold me to the late Sultan?

CONDEMNED MAN: Yes.

SULTAN: When was that?

CONDEMNED MAN: Twenty-five years ago, Your Majesty. You were a small boy of six, lost and abandoned in a Circassian village raided by the Mongols. You were extremely intelligent and wise for one of your tender years. I rejoiced in you and carried you off to the Sultan of this country. As the price for you he made me a present of one thousand dinars.

SULTAN (*derisively*): Only a thousand dinars!

CONDEMNED MAN: Of course you were worth more than that but I was new to the trade, not being more than twenty-six years of age. That deal was the beginning of my business – it opened for me the way to the future.

SULTAN: For you and for me!

CONDEMNED MAN: Thanks be to God!

SULTAN: Is it this that merits your death – bringing me to this country? I see the matter quite differently.

VIZIER: He deserves death for his babbling and indiscretion.

SULTAN: I see no great harm in his saying or bruiting abroad the fact that I was a slave. The late Sultan was just that – is not that right, Vizier?

VIZIER: That's right but . . .

SULTAN: Is it not so, Chief Cadi?

VIZIER: Quite so, O Sultan.

SULTAN: The entire family comes from slaves since time
    immemorial. The Mameluke Sultans were all taken from
    earliest childhood to the palace, there to be given a strict
    and hardy upbringing; and later they became rulers, army
    leaders, and Sultans of countries. I am merely one of those,
    in no way different from them.

CONDEMNED MAN: Rather are you among the best of them in
    wisdom and sound judgement, may God preserve you for the
    good of your subjects.

SULTAN: Even so, I don't remember your face; in fact I don't
    clearly remember my childhood days in that Circassian
    village you talk about and in which you say you found me.
    All I remember is my childhood at the palace under the
    protection of the late Sultan. He used to treat me as though
    I were his real son, for he himself had no children. He
    brought me up and instructed me so that I might take over
    the rule. I knew for absolute certainty that he was not my
    father.

CONDEMNED MAN: Your parents were killed by the Mongols.

SULTAN: No one ever talked to me of my parents. I knew only
    that I had been brought to the palace at a young age.

CONDEMNED MAN: And it was I who brought you there.

SULTAN: Maybe.

CONDEMNED MAN: Therefore, Your Majesty, what is my crime?

SULTAN: By God, I know not. Ask him who accused you.

VIZIER: That's not his real crime.

SULTAN: Is there a real crime?

VIZIER: Yes, Your Majesty. To say that you had been a slave is
    truly not something shameful, no reason for guilt – all the
    Mameluke Sultans have been slaves. It's not there that the
    crime lies. However, a Mameluke Sultan is generally
    manumitted before ascending the throne.

SULTAN: So what?

VIZIER: So, Your Majesty, this man claims that you have not yet
    been manumitted, that you are still a slave and that a
    person bearing such a stigma is not entitled to rule over a
    free people.

SULTAN (*to the condemned man*): Did you really say this?

CONDEMNED MAN: I did not say all that; however, people in the
    market place always enjoy such gossip and tittle-tattle.

SULTAN: And from where did you learn that I had not been
    manumitted?

CONDEMNED MAN: It is not I who said so. They ascribe to me every infamous word that is spoken.

SULTAN: But they are nevertheless indulging in gossip and tittle-tattle.

CONDEMNED MAN: Not I.

SULTAN: You or someone else – it no longer matters. The important thing now is that all the people everywhere know that it is all sheer lies – isn't that so, Chief Cadi?

CADI: The fact is, Your Majesty . . .

SULTAN: It's utter falsehood and slander. It's mere fabrication unsupported by logic or common sense. Not yet manumitted? I? I, who was a leader of armies and conquered the Mongols? I, the right-hand man of the late Sultan, whom he arranged to rule after him? All this, and the Sultan did not think about manumitting me before his death? Is it plausible? Listen, Cadi! All you now have to do is to let the town-criers announce an official denial in the city and publish to the people the text of the document registering my manumission, which is doubtless kept in your strong-rooms, isn't that so?

CADI (combing his fingers through his beard): You are saying, Your Majesty . . .

SULTAN: Didn't you hear what I said?

CADI: Yes, but . . .

SULTAN: You were busy playing with your beard.

CADI: Your Majesty!

SULTAN: What? Your Majesty the Sultan is addressing you in clear and simple language requiring no long consideration or deep thought. All it amounts to is that it has become necessary to make public the document. Do you understand?

CADI: Yes.

SULTAN: You're still playing with your beard. Can't you leave it alone – just for a while?

VIZIER (intervening): Your Majesty! Would you permit me . . .

SULTAN: What's up with you? You too?

VIZIER: I would ask Your Majesty to . . .

SULTAN: What's all this embarrassment? You and he are as bad as each other.

CADI: It is better to postpone this trial until some other time – when we are on our own, Your Majesty.

VIZIER: Yes, that would be best.

SULTAN: I'm beginning to catch on.

The Vizier, by a sign, orders everyone to move off with the
condemned man, leaving only himself, the Sultan, and the Chief Cadi
on stage.

SULTAN: Now here we are on our own. What have you to say?
I see from your expressions that you have things to say.

CADI: Yes, Your Majesty. You have with your perspicacity
realized . . . in actual fact there is no document of your
manumission in my strong-rooms.

SULTAN: Perhaps you have not yet received it, though it must be
somewhere. Isn't that so, Vizier?

VIZIER: In truth, Your Majesty . . .

SULTAN: What?

VIZIER: The truth is that . . .

SULTAN: Speak!

VIZIER: There is no document to prove your having been
manumitted.

SULTAN: What are you saying?

VIZIER: The late Sultan collapsed suddenly following a heart
attack and departed this life before manumitting you.

SULTAN: What's this you're alleging, you rogue?

VIZIER: I'm certainly a rogue, Your Majesty – and a criminal.
I'm wicked, I don't deny it. I should have arranged all this
at the time, but this business of manumission did not occur to
me. My head was filled with other weighty matters. At that
time, Your Majesty, you were far away – in the thick of the
fray. No one but myself was present by the dying Sultan's
bedside. I forgot this matter under the stress of the situation,
the momentous nature of the occasion, and the intensity of
my grief. Nothing occupied me at that moment save taking
the oath, before the dying man, that I would serve you, Your
Majesty, with the very same devotion as that with which I
had served him for the whole of his life.

SULTAN: Truly, here and now you have really served me!

VIZIER: I deserve death – I know that. It is an unpardonable
crime. The late Sultan could not think of everything or
remember everything. It was the very essence of my work to
think for him and to remind him of important matters. It
was certainly my duty to put before him the matter of
manumission, because of its particular seriousness, and to do
the necessary legal formalities. But your lofty position, Your
Majesty, your influence, your prestige, your great place in

people's hearts — all these high attributes caused us to overlook your being a slave; to overlook the necessity for someone of your stature to have such proofs and documents. I swear to God, this matter never occurred to me until after you had ascended the throne, Your Majesty. At that time the whole business became clear to me. I was seized with terror and almost went mad. I would surely have done so, had I not calmed down and pulled myself together, cherishing the hope that this matter would never arise or be revealed.

SULTAN: And now it has arisen and been revealed.

VIZIER: What a tragedy! I did not know that such a man would come along one day with his gossip and tittle-tattle.

SULTAN: For this reason you wanted to close his mouth by handing him over to the executioner?

VIZIER: Yes.

SULTAN: And so bury your fault by burying the man himself?

VIZIER (*with head lowered*): Yes.

SULTAN: And what's the point of that now? Everyone's gossiping now.

VIZIER: If this man's head were cut off and hung up in the square before the people, no tongue would thenceforth dare to utter.

SULTAN: Do you think so?

VIZIER: If the sword is not able to cut off tongues, then what can?

CADI: Will you allow me to say a word, Your Majesty?

SULTAN: I'm listening.

CADI: The sword certainly does away with heads and tongues; it does not, however, do away with difficulties and problems.

SULTAN: What do you mean?

CADI: I mean that the problem will still nevertheless remain, namely that the Sultan is ruling without having been manumitted, and that a slave is at the head of a free people.

VIZIER: Who dares to say this? Whoever does so will have his head cut off.

CADI: That's another question.

VIZIER: It is not necessary for the person ruling to be carrying around documents and proofs. We have the strongest and most striking example of this in the Fatimid dynasty. Every one of us remembers what Al-Mu'izz li-Din Allah Al-Fatimi did. One day he came along claiming he was descended from the Prophet (the prayers of God be upon

him), and when the people did not believe him, he went at
them with drawn sword and opened up his coffers of gold,
saying 'These are my forbears, these my ancestors'. The
people kept silent and he reigned and his children reigned
after him quietly and peaceably for centuries long.

SULTAN: What do you say about this, Cadi?

CADI: I say that this is correct from the historical point of view
but . . .

SULTAN: But what?

CADI: Then, O illustrious Sultan, you would like to solve your
problem by this method?

SULTAN: And why not?

VIZIER: Truly, why not? There is nothing easier than this,
especially in this matter of ours. It is sufficient for us to
announce publicly that Our Majesty the Sultan has been
legally manumitted, that he was manumitted by the late
Sultan before his death, and that the documents and proofs
are recorded and kept with the Chief Cadi – and death to
anyone who dares deny it!

CADI: There is a person who will so deny.

VIZIER: Who's that?

CADI: I.

SULTAN: You?

CADI: Yes, Your Majesty. I cannot take part in this conspiracy.

VIZIER: It is not a conspiracy – it's a plan for saving the
situation.

CADI: It is a conspiracy against the law I represent.

SULTAN: The law?

CADI: Yes, Sultan – the law. In the eyes of the civil and religious
codes you are only a slave, and a slave – by civil and religious
law – is regarded as a thing, a chattel. As the late Sultan,
who had the power of life and death over you, did not
manumit you before his death, you are thus still a thing, a
chattel, owned by someone else, and so you have forfeited
the basic qualification for entering into the normal
transactions exercised by the rest of free people.

SULTAN: Is this the law?

CADI: Yes.

VIZIER: Take it easy, Chief Cadi! We are not now discussing the
view of the law but are looking for a way by which to be free
of this law, and the way to be free of it is to assume that
manumission has in fact taken place. So long as the matter

is a secret between us three, with no one but ourselves knowing the truth, it will be easy to induce the people to believe . . .

CADI: The lie.

VIZIER: The solution rather – it's a more appropriate and suitable word.

CADI: A solution through lying.

VIZIER: And what's the harm in that?

CADI: In relation to you two there is no harm.

VIZIER: And in relation to you?

CADI: In relation to me it's different, for I cannot fool myself and I cannot free myself from the law, being as I am the person who represents it; I cannot break an oath by which I took upon myself to be the trusted servant of the civil and religious law.

SULTAN: You took this upon yourself before me.

CADI: And before God and my conscience.

SULTAN: Which means that you won't go along with us?

CADI: Along this road, no.

SULTAN: You will not join hands with us?

CADI: In this instance, no.

SULTAN: Then in that case you can take yourself off to one side. Don't interfere in anything and leave us to act as we think fit. You thus keep your oath and satisfy your conscience.

CADI: I'm sorry, Your Majesty.

SULTAN: Why?

CADI: Because, having admitted that in the eyes of the law you are lacking the authority to make a contract, I find myself obliged to order that all your actions are null and void.

SULTAN: You're mad – that's impossible!

CADI: I'm sorry but I cannot do other than this so long as . . .

SULTAN: So long as?

CADI: So long as you don't order me to be dismissed from my post, thrown out of the country, or have my head cut off. In this manner I would be freed from my oath and you could suit yourself and do as you pleased.

SULTAN: Is this a threat?

CADI: No, it's a solution.

VIZIER: You're complicating the problem for us, Chief Cadi.

CADI: I am helping you to get out of an impasse.

SULTAN: I've begun to weary of this man.

VIZIER: He knows that we are in his grasp in that he will divulge everything to the people if the least amount of coercion is used on him.

SULTAN (*to the Cadi*): The substance of what you say is that you don't want to assist us.

CADI: On the contrary, Your Majesty, I wish very greatly to be of assistance to you, but *not* in this manner.

SULTAN: What do you suggest then?

CADI: That the law be applied.

SULTAN: If *you* applied the law, *I'd* lose my throne.

CADI: Not only that.

SULTAN: Is there something even worse?

CADI: Yes.

SULTAN: What is there then?

CADI: Owing to the fact that in the eyes of the law you are a chattel owned by the late Sultan, you have become part of his inheritance, and as he died without leaving an heir, his estate reverts to the Exchequer. You are thus one of the chattels owned by the Exchequer – an unproductive chattel yielding no profit or return. I, in my additional capacity as Treasurer of the Exchequer, say: it is the custom in such cases to get rid of unprofitable chattels by putting them up for sale at auction, so that the good interests of the Exchequer be not harmed and so that it may utilize the proceeds of the sale in bringing benefit to the people generally and in particular to the poor.

SULTAN (*indignantly*): An unproductive chattel? I?

CADI: I am speaking of course strictly from the legal point of view.

SULTAN: Up until now I have obtained no solutions from you. All I have had are insults.

CADI: Insults? I beg your pardon, illustrious Sultan. You know very well how much I revere and admire you and in what high esteem I hold you. You will recollect no doubt that it was I who from the first moment was the one to come forward to pay you homage and proclaim you as the Sultan to rule over our country. What I am doing now is merely to give a frank review of the situation from the point of view of civil and religious law.

SULTAN: The long and short of it is then that I'm a thing and a chattel and not a man or a human being?

CADI: Yes.

SULTAN: And that this thing or chattel is owned by the Exchequer?

CADI: Indeed.

SULTAN: And that the Exchequer disposes of unproductive chattels by putting them up for sale at auction for the public good?

CADI: Exactly.

SULTAN: Oh Chief Cadi, don't you feel, as I do, that this is all extraordinarily bizarre?

CADI: Yes, but . . .

SULTAN: And that there's a great deal of undue exaggeration and extravagance in it all?

CADI: Maybe, but in my capacity as Cadi what concerns me is where the facts stand in relation to the processes of the law.

SULTAN: Listen, Cadi. This law of yours has brought me no solution, whereas a small movement of my sword will ensure that the knot of the problem is severed instantly.

CADI: Then do so.

SULTAN: I shall. What does the spilling of a little blood matter for the sake of the practicability of governing?

CADI: Then you must start by spilling my blood.

SULTAN: I shall do everything I think necessary for safeguarding the security of the State, and I shall in fact start with you. I shall cast you into prison. Vizier! Arrest the Cadi!

VIZIER: Your Majesty, you have not yet listened to his answer to your question.

SULTAN: What question?

VIZIER: The question about the solution he deems appropriate for the problem.

SULTAN: He has answered this question.

VIZIER: What he said was not the solution but a review of the situation.

SULTAN: Is that true, Cadi?

CADI: Yes.

SULTAN: Have you then a solution to this problem of ours?

CADI (in the same tone): Yes.

SULTAN: Then speak! What is the solution?

CADI: There is only one solution.

SULTAN: Say! What is it?

CADI: That the law be applied.

SULTAN: Again? Once more?

CADI: Yes – once more and always, for I see no other solution.

SULTAN: Do you hear, Vizier? After this, do you entertain any hope of co-operation with this stubborn old windbag?

VIZIER: Allow me, Your Majesty, to interrogate him a little.

SULTAN: Do as you like!

VIZIER: O Chief Cadi, the question is a subtle one and it requires of you to explain to us clearly and in detail your point of view.

CADI: My point of view is both clear and simple and I can propound it in two words: for the solution of this problem we have before us two alternatives, that of the sword and that of the law. As for the sword, that is none of my concern; as for the law, that is what it behoves me to recommend and on which I can give a legal opinion. The law says: it is only his master, the possessor of the power of life and death over him, who has the right to manumit a slave. In this instance, the master, the possessor of the power of life and death, died without leaving an heir and the ownership of the slave has reverted to the Exchequer. The Exchequer may not manumit him without compensation in that no one has the right to dispose gratis of property or chattels belonging to the State. It is, however, permitted for the Exchequer to make a disposition by sale, and the selling of the property of the State is not valid by law other than by an auction carried out publicly. The legal solution, therefore, is that we should put up His Majesty the Sultan for sale by public auction and the person to whom he is knocked down thereafter manumits him. In this manner the Exchequer is not harmed or defrauded in respect of its property and the Sultan gains his manumission and release through the law.

SULTAN (to the Vizier): Do you hear all this?

VIZIER (to the Cadi): We put up Our Majesty, the illustrious Sultan, for sale by public auction! This is sheer madness!

CADI: This is the legal and legitimate solution.

SULTAN (to the Vizier): Don't waste time. No answer is left for this stupid and impudent fellow except to chop off his head – and let result what may! And it is I who shall perform this with my own hand. (He draws his sword.)

CADI: It is a great honour for me, Your Majesty, to die by your hand and for me to give up my life for the sake of truth and principles.

VIZIER: Patience, Your Majesty, patience! Don't make a martyr of this man! Such a broken-down old man could not hope for

a more splendid death. It will be said that through him you
destroyed the civil and religious laws; he will become the
living symbol of the spirit of truth and principles – and many
a glorious martyr has more effect and influence on the
conscience of peoples than a tyrannical king.

SULTAN (*suppressing his anger*): God's curse . . .

VIZIER: Don't give him this glory, Your Majesty, at the expense
of the situation.

SULTAN: Then what's to be done? This man puts us in a dilemma,
he makes us choose between two alternatives, both of them
painful: the law which shows me up as weak and makes a
laughing-stock of me, or the sword which brands me with
brutality and makes me loathed.

VIZIER (*turning to the Cadi*): O Chief Cadi! Be tractable and
obliging! Don't be rigid and hard! Meet us half-way, find a
compromise and work with us towards finding a reasonable
solution.

CADI: There is no reasonable way out other than the law.

VIZIER: We put the Sultan up for sale by auction?

CADI: Yes.

VIZIER: And the person he's knocked down to buys him?

CADI: He manumits him immediately, at the session for drawing
up the contract – that's the condition.

VIZIER: And who will accept to lose his money in this manner?

CADI: Many people – those who would ransom the Sultan's
freedom with their money.

VIZIER: Then why don't we ourselves undertake this duty – you
and I – and ransom our Sultan secretly with our own money
and gain this honour? Is it not an appropriate idea?

CADI: I'm afraid not. It cannot be secret – the law is specific in
that it lays down that every sale of the properties of the
Exchequer must be carried out publicly and by general
auction.

SULTAN (*to the Vizier*): Don't trouble yourself with him – he's
determined to disgrace us.

VIZIER (*to the Cadi*): For the last time, Chief Cadi – is there no
stratagem for extracting us from this impasse?

CADI: A stratagem? I am not the person to ask to look for
stratagems.

SULTAN: Naturally! This man looks only for what will provoke
and humiliate us.

CADI: Not I as a person, Your Majesty. I as a person am weak and have nothing to do with the whole matter. If the matter were in my hands and depended upon my wishes, I would like nothing better than to extricate you from this situation in the best manner you could wish.

SULTAN: Poor weak fellow! The matter's not in his hands – in whose hands then?

CADI: The law's.

SULTAN: Yes, the spectre behind which he hides in order to subjugate me, impose his will upon me, and show me up before the people in that laughable, feeble, and ignominious guise.

CADI: I as a person would rather wish for you to appear in the guise of the glorious ruler.

SULTAN: Do you consider it as being among the characteristics of glory that a sultan be treated like goods or chattels to be sold in the market?

CADI: It is certainly a characteristic of glory that a sultan should submit to the law as do the rest of people.

VIZIER: It is truly laudable, Chief Cadi, that the ruler should obey the law as does the sentenced person, but this entails a great hazard. The politics of government have their procedures; the ruling of people has other methods.

CADI: I know nothing of politics or of the business of ruling people.

SULTAN: It's our business – allow us then to exercise it in our own way.

CADI: I have not fettered your hands, Your Majesty. You possess complete freedom to exercise your rule as you wish.

SULTAN: Fine! I now see what I must do.

VIZIER: What are you going to do, Your Majesty?

SULTAN: Look at this old man! Do you see him carrying a sword on his belt? Of course not. He carries nothing but a tongue in his mouth with which he turns words and phrases. He's good at using the acumen and skill he possesses, but I carry this (*and he indicates his sword*). It's not made of wood, it's not a toy. It's a real sword and must be useful for something, must have some reason for its existence. Do you understand what I'm saying? Answer! Why was it ordained that I should carry it? Is it for decoration or for action?

VIZIER: For action.

SULTAN: And you, Cadi – why do you not answer? Answer! Is it for decoration or for action?

CADI: For one or the other.

SULTAN: What are you saying?

CADI: I am saying, for this or for that.

SULTAN: What do you mean?

CADI: I mean that you have a choice, Your Majesty. You can employ it for action, or you can employ it for decoration. I recognize the undoubted strength possessed by the sword, its swift action and decisive effect. But the sword gives right to the strongest, and who knows who will be the strongest tomorrow? There may appear some strong person who will tilt the balance of power against you. As for the law, it protects your rights from every aggression, because it does not recognize the strongest – it recognizes right. And now there's nothing for you to do, Your Majesty, but choose: between the sword which imposes and yet exposes you, and between the law which threatens and yet protects you.

SULTAN (*thinking a while*): The sword which imposes and exposes me, and the law which threatens and protects me?

CADI: Yes.

SULTAN: What talk is this?

CADI: The frank truth.

SULTAN (*thinking and repeating over to himself*): The sword which imposes and exposes? The law which threatens and protects?

CADI: Yes, Your Majesty.

SULTAN (*to the Vizier*): What an accursed old man he is! He's got a unique genius for always landing us in a spot.

CADI: I have done nothing, Your Majesty, except to present to you the two sides of the question; the choice is yours.

SULTAN: The choice? The choice? What is your opinion, Vizier?

VIZIER: It is for you to decide about this, Your Majesty.

SULTAN: As far as I can see, you don't know either.

VIZIER: Actually, Your Majesty, the . . .

SULTAN: The choice is difficult?

VIZIER: Certainly.

SULTAN: The sword which imposes me on all and yet which exposes me to danger, or the law which threatens my wishes yet which protects my rights.

VIZIER: Yes.

SULTAN: You choose for me.

VIZIER: I? No, no, Your Majesty!

SULTAN: What are you frightened of?

VIZIER: Of the consequences – of the consequences of this choice.

Should it one day become apparent that I had chosen the wrong course, then what a catastrophe there'd be!

SULTAN: You don't want to bear the responsibility?

VIZIER: I wouldn't dare – it's not my right.

SULTAN: In the end a decision must be made.

VIZIER: No one, Your Majesty, but yourself has the right to decide in this matter.

SULTAN: Truly, there is no one but myself. I cannot escape from that. It's I who must choose and bear the responsibility of the choice.

VIZIER: You are our master and our ruler.

SULTAN: Yes, this is my most fearful moment, the fearful moment for every ruler – the moment of giving the final decision, the decision that will change the course of things, the moment when is uttered that small word which will decide the inevitable choice, the choice that will decide fate.

He thinks hard as he walks up and down, with the other two waiting for him to speak. Silence reigns for a moment.

SULTAN (*with head lowered in thought*): The sword or the law? The law or the sword?

VIZIER: Your Majesty, I appreciate the precariousness of your situation.

SULTAN: Yet you don't want to assist me with an opinion?

VIZIER: I cannot. In this situation you alone are the one to decide.

SULTAN: There is, therefore, no getting away from deciding all by myself?

VIZIER: That's so.

SULTAN: The sword or the law? The law or the sword? (*He thinks for a while, then raises his head sharply.*) Good – I've decided.

VIZIER: Let us have your orders, Your Majesty.

SULTAN: I have decided to choose, to choose . . .

VIZIER: What, Your Majesty?

SULTAN (*shouting decisively*): The law! I have chosen the law!

CURTAIN

Act Two

The same square. Guards have started to arrange rows of people around a platform that has been set up there. The Wine Merchant's shop is closed and he is standing talking to the Shoemaker, who is engrossed in his work at the open door of his shop.

WINE MERCHANT: How odd of you, Shoemaker! You open your shop and work when today every shop is closed, just like a feast day?

SHOEMAKER: And why should I close it? Is it because they're selling the Sultan?

WINE MERCHANT: You fool – because you'll be watching the most incredible sight in the world!

SHOEMAKER: I can see everything that goes on from here while I work.

WINE MERCHANT: It's up to you. As for me I've closed my shop so that I shan't miss the smallest detail of this wonderful spectacle.

SHOEMAKER: You're making the biggest mistake, my friend. Today's an excellent opportunity for attracting customers. It's not every day you get such crowds gathered outside your shop. It is certain that today many people will suffer from thirst and will yearn for a drop of your drink.

WINE MERCHANT: Do you think so?

SHOEMAKER: It's obvious. Look – here am I, for example, showing off my finest shoes today. (*He points to the shoes hanging up at the door of his shop.*)

WINE MERCHANT: My dear Shoemaker, those who come to buy today have come to buy the Sultan, not your shoes.

SHOEMAKER: Why not? Maybe there are some among the people who are in greater need of my shoes.

WINE MERCHANT: Shut up, say no more! It seems you don't understand what's so extraordinary about this happening, don't realize that it's unique. Do you find a sultan being put up for sale every day?

SHOEMAKER: Listen, friend. I'll talk to you frankly: even were I
    to have sufficient money to buy the Sultan, by God I
    wouldn't do it!

WINE MERCHANT: You wouldn't buy him?

SHOEMAKER: Never!

WINE MERCHANT: Allow me to say you're a fool!

SHOEMAKER: No, I'm intelligent and astute. Just tell me what
    you'd want me to do with a sultan in my shop? Can I teach
    him this trade of mine? Of course not! Can I entrust him
    with any work? Certainly not! Then, it's I who'll go on
    working doubly hard so as to feed him, look after him, and
    serve him. I swear that that is what would happen. I'd
    merely be buying a rod for my back, a sheer luxury I
    couldn't afford. My resources, friend, don't allow me to
    acquire works of art.

WINE MERCHANT: What nonsense!

SHOEMAKER: And you – would you buy him?

WINE MERCHANT: Can there be any doubt about that?

SHOEMAKER: What would you do with him?

WINE MERCHANT: Many things, very many things, my friend. His
    mere presence in my shop would be enough to bring along
    the whole city. It would be enough to ask him to recount to
    my customers every evening the stories of his battles against
    the Mongols, the strange things that have happened to him,
    his voyages and adventures, the countries he has seen, the
    places he's been to, the deserts he's crossed – wouldn't all
    that be valuable and enjoyable?

SHOEMAKER: Certainly, you could employ him in that manner
    but I . . .

WINE MERCHANT: You too could do the same.

SHOEMAKER: How? He knows nothing about repairing shoes or
    making soles for him to be able to talk about them.

WINE MERCHANT: It's not necessary for him to talk in your shop.

SHOEMAKER: What would he do then?

WINE MERCHANT: If I were in your place I'd know how to
    employ him.

SHOEMAKER: How? Tell me.

WINE MERCHANT: I'd sit him down in front of the door of the
    shop in a comfortable chair, I'd put a new pair of shoes on
    his feet and a placard above his head reading: 'Sultan Shoes
    Sold Here', and the next day you'd see how the people of the
    city would flock to your shop and demand your wares.

SHOEMAKER: What a great idea!

WINE MERCHANT: Isn't it?

SHOEMAKER: I'm beginning to admire your ingenuity.

WINE MERCHANT: What do you say then to thinking about buying him together and making him our joint property. I'd release him to you during the day and you could give him to me for the evening?

SHOEMAKER: A lovely dream! But all we own, you and I, isn't enough to buy one of his fingers.

WINE MERCHANT: That's true.

SHOEMAKER: Look! The crowds have begun to arrive and collect.

Groups of men, women and children gather together and chat among themselves.

FIRST MAN (*to another man*): Is it here they'll be selling the Sultan?

SECOND MAN: Yes, don't you see the guards?

FIRST MAN: If only I had money!

SECOND MAN: Shut up! That's for the rich!

CHILD: Mother! Is that the Sultan?

MOTHER (*to the child*): No, child, that's one of the guards.

CHILD: Where is the Sultan then?

MOTHER: He hasn't come yet.

CHILD: Has the Sultan got a sword?

MOTHER: Yes, a large sword.

CHILD: And will they sell him here?

MOTHER: Yes, child.

CHILD: When, Mother?

MOTHER: Very soon.

CHILD: Mother! Buy him for me!

MOTHER: What?

CHILD: The Sultan! Buy me the Sultan!

MOTHER: Quiet! He's not a toy for you to play with.

CHILD: You said they'll sell him here. Buy him for me then.

MOTHER: Quiet, child. This is not a game for children.

CHILD: For whom then? For grown-ups?

MOTHER: Yes, it's for grown-ups.

The window of the Lady's house is opened and the maidservant looks out.

MAID (*calling*): Wine Merchant! Tavern keeper! Have you closed your shop today?

WINE MERCHANT: Yes – haven't I done right? And your mistress? Where is she? Is she still in bed?

MAID: No, she has just got out of her bath to dress.

WINE MERCHANT: She was superb! Her trick with the Executioner worked well.

MAID: Quiet! He's there. I can see him in the crowd. Now he's spotted us.

EXECUTIONER (*approaching the Wine Merchant*): God curse you and wine!

WINE MERCHANT: Why? What sin has my wine committed to justify your curse? Didn't it bring joy to your heart that night, stimulate you in your singing, and cause you to see everything around you clear and pure?

EXECUTIONER (*in tones of anger*): Clear and pure! Certainly that night I saw everything clear and pure!

WINE MERCHANT: Certainly – do you doubt it?

EXECUTIONER: Shut up and don't remind me of that night.

WINE MERCHANT: I've shut up. Tell me: are you on holiday today?

EXECUTIONER: Yes.

WINE MERCHANT: And your friend the condemned man?

EXECUTIONER: He has been pardoned.

WINE MERCHANT: And you, naturally. No one asked you about that business at dawn?

EXECUTIONER: No.

WINE MERCHANT: Then everything has turned out for the best.

EXECUTIONER: Yes, but I don't like anyone to make a fool of me or play tricks on me.

MAID: Even when it means saving a man's head?

EXECUTIONER: Shut up, you vile woman – you and your mistress.

MAID: Are you continuing to insult us on such a day?

WINE MERCHANT (*to the Executioner*): Don't upset yourself! This evening I'll bring you a large glass of the best wine – free.

EXECUTIONER: Free?

WINE MERCHANT: Yes, a present from me, to drink to the health . . .

EXECUTIONER: Of whom?

WINE MERCHANT (*catching sight of the Muezzin approaching*): To the health of the brave Muezzin!

EXECUTIONER: That most evil of liars!

MUEZZIN: A liar? Me?

EXECUTIONER: Yes, you claim that I was fast asleep at that hour.

MUEZZIN: And you were drunk!

EXECUTIONER: I'm absolutely convinced that I was awake and alert and that I hadn't slept for a moment up until then.

MUEZZIN: So long as *you're* absolutely convinced of that . . .

EXECUTIONER: Yes, I didn't sleep at all up until then.

MUEZZIN: Fine!

EXECUTIONER: You mean you agree about that?

MUEZZIN: Yes.

EXECUTIONER: Then it's you who're lying.

MUEZZIN: No!

EXECUTIONER: Then I *was* sleeping?

MUEZZIN: Yes.

EXECUTIONER: How can you say yes?

MUEZZIN: No!

EXECUTIONER: Make your mind up! Is it yes or is it no?

MUEZZIN: Which do you want?

EXECUTIONER: I want to know whether I was asleep at that time or whether I was awake.

MUEZZIN: What does it matter to you? So long as everything has passed peacefully – your friend the condemned man has been issued with a pardon and no one has asked you about anything. As for me, no one has spoken to me about the matter of that dawn. The question in relation to us all has ended as well as we could hope, so why dig up the past?

EXECUTIONER: Yes, but the question still troubles me since that day. I haven't grasped the situation absolutely clearly. I want to know whether I really was asleep at that time and whether you really gave the call to the dawn prayer without my being aware of it. In the end you must divulge to me what actually happened for you doubtless know the whole truth. Tell me exactly what happened then. I was in truth a little drunk at the time but . . .

MUEZZIN: Since the matter occupies your mind to such an extent, why should I put you at ease. I prefer to leave you like this, grilling away and turning on the fire of doubt.

EXECUTIONER: May you turn on Hell's Fire, you ruffian of a Muezzin!

MUEZZIN (*shouting*): Look! Look! The Sultan's retinue has come!

The retinue with the Sultan at its head appears, followed by the Chief Cadi, the Vizier, and the condemned slave trader. They walk towards the dais, where the Sultan seats himself in the middle chair with all around him, while the slave trader stands beside him to face the people.

WINE MERCHANT (*to the Executioner*): Extraordinary! This is your friend the condemned man. What has brought him here alongside the Sultan?

EXECUTIONER (*looking at him*): Truly, by God, it's none other than he.

MUEZZIN: No doubt he is the person charged with making the sale – is he not one of the biggest slave traders?

WINE MERCHANT: Do you see, Executioner? His escape, therefore, from your hands was no accident.

EXECUTIONER: How extraordinary! Here he is selling the same sultan twice – once as a child and again now when he's grown up.

MUEZZIN: Quiet! He's about to talk.

SLAVE TRADER (*clapping his hands*): Quiet, people! I announce to you, in my capacity of slave-trader and auctioneer, that I have been charged with carrying out this sale by public auction for the benefit of the Exchequer. It honours me, first of all, that the Chief Cadi will open these proceedings with a word explaining the conditions of this sale. Let our venerable Chief Cadi now speak.

CADI: O people! The sale to be held before you is not like any other sale: it is of a special kind and this fact has been previously announced to you. This sale must be accompanied by another contract, a contract of manumission whereby the person who is the highest bidder at the auction may not retain what he has bought but must proceed with the manumission at the same session as the contract of sale, that is to say at this present session of ours. There is no need for me to remind you of the law's provision which prevents State employees from participating in any sale by the State. Having said this I leave the Vizier to speak to you about the patriotic character of these proceedings.

SHOEMAKER (*whispering to the Wine Merchant*): Did you hear? The buyer cannot keep what he has bought. This means throwing one's money into the sea.

WINE MERCHANT (*whispering*): We'll now see what imbecile will
    come forward.

SLAVE TRADER: Silence! Silence!

VIZIER: Honourable people! You are today present at a great
    and unique occasion, one of the most important in our history:
    a glorious Sultan asks for his freedom and has recourse to his
    people instead of to his sword – that sharp and mighty
    sword by which he was victorious in battles against the
    Mongols and with which he could also have been victorious in
    gaining his freedom and liberating himself from slavery. But
    our just and triumphant Sultan has chosen to submit to the
    law like the lowliest individual amongst his subjects. Here
    he is seeking his freedom by the method laid down by law.
    Whoever of you wishes to redeem the freedom of his beloved
    Sultan, let him come forward to this auction, and whoever of
    you pays the highest price will have done a goodly act for
    his homeland and will be remembered for time immemorial.

Cheers from the crowd.

VOICE (*raised from amongst the people*): Long live the Sultan!

ANOTHER VOICE: Long live the law!

SLAVE TRADER: Silence, O people!

VIZIER (*continuing*): And now, O noble people, that you know
    the small and trivial sacrifice your country expects of you for
    the sake of this high and lofty purpose – the freeing of your
    Sultan with your money and the passing of that money to the
    Exchequer so that it may be spent on the poor and those in
    need – now that your dearly beloved and cherished Sultan
    has come to you so that you may compete in showing your
    appreciation of him and liberating him, I declare that the
    proceedings shall begin.

*He indicates to the Slave Trader that he should begin, while the
crowds cheer.*

SLAVE TRADER: Silence! Silence! O people of this city, the
    auction has commenced. I shall not resort to enumerating
    properties and attributes as is generally resorted to in the
    markets for the purpose of making people want to acquire the
    goods, for the subject of this sale is above every description or
    comment. It is no extravagance or exaggeration to say that

he is worth his weight in gold. However, it is not the intention to make things difficult or to inhibit you, but to facilitate matters for you in gauging what is possible. I thus begin the auction with a sum both small and paltry in respect of a sultan: Ten thousand dinars! (*Uproar amongst the crowd.*)

SHOEMAKER (*to the Wine Merchant*): Ten thousand? Only! What a trifling sum! Look at that great ruby in his turban! By God, it alone is worth a hundred thousand dinars!

WINE MERCHANT: Truly it's a paltry amount – especially when paid for a noble and patriotic end! Ten thousand dinars! It is not seemly. I'm a loyal citizen and this displeases me. (*shouts*) Eleven thousand dinars!

SLAVE TRADER: Eleven thousand dinars! Eleven thousand?

SHOEMAKER (*to the Wine Merchant*): Only eleven thousand dinars? Is that all you have? Then I'll say (*shouting*) – twelve thousand dinars!

SLAVE TRADER: Twelve thousand dinars! Twelve thousand . . .

WINE MERCHANT (*to the Shoemaker*): Are you outbidding me? Then I'll say . . . thirteen thousand dinars!

SLAVE TRADER: Thirteen thousand dinars! Thirteen thousand . . .

An unknown man comes forward suddenly, forcing his way through the crowd.

UNKNOWN MAN (*shouting*): Fifteen thousand dinars!

SHOEMAKER: Good heavens! Who can this man be?

WINE MERCHANT: A joker of your own ilk without doubt.

SHOEMAKER: And of your ilk too.

SLAVE TRADER: Fifteen thousand dinars! Fifteen thousand! Fifteen thousand!

SHOEMAKER (*shouting*): Sixteen thousand dinars!

SLAVE TRADER (*shouting*): Sixteen thousand dinars! Sixteen!

UNKNOWN MAN: Eighteen thousand dinars!

SHOEMAKER (*to the Wine Merchant*): In one fell swoop! This fellow's overdoing things!

SLAVE TRADER: Eighteen thousand dinars! Eighteen thousand!

WINE MERCHANT (*scrutinizing the unknown man closely*): It seems to me I've seen this man somewhere. Yes, he's one of the well-to-do; he comes to my tavern from time to time and drinks a glass of wine before going up to that beautiful lady.

SHOEMAKER (*turning to her window*): Look! There she is at the

window! Glittering in all her cheap finery as though she
were some sugar doll! (*Shouts to her*) You pretty one up in
your heights, are you too not a loyal citizen?

LADY: Shut up, you Shoemaker! I am not one to be made fun of
in such circumstances. By God, if you don't keep quiet I'll
tell on you and they'll put you into prison.

SLAVE TRADER (*calling out*): Eighteen thousand dinars ... at a
sum of eighteen thousand ...

A leading citizen comes forward to the dais.

CITIZEN (*shouting*): Nineteen thousand dinars!

UNKNOWN MAN: I bid twenty thousand dinars!

SLAVE TRADER: Twenty thousand dinars! Twenty thousand
dinars! Twenty!

CITIZEN: I bid twenty-one thousand dinars!

UNKNOWN MAN: Twenty-two thousand dinars!

A second leading citizen comes forward.

2ND CITIZEN: Twenty-three thousand dinars!

SLAVE TRADER: Twenty-three! Twenty-three!

UNKNOWN MAN: Twenty-five!

SLAVE TRADER: Twenty-five thousand dinars! Twenty-five!

A third leading citizen comes forward.

3RD CITIZEN: Twenty-six!

SLAVE TRADER (*shouting*): Twenty-six thousand dinars! Twenty-
six!

UNKNOWN MAN: Twenty-eight!

SLAVE TRADER (*shouting*): Twenty-eight! Twenty-eight thousand
dinars!

3RD CITIZEN: Twenty-nine!

SHOEMAKER (*whispering to the Wine Merchant*): Are these people
really serious about all this?

WINE MERCHANT: It seems so.

SLAVE TRADER: Twenty-nine ... twenty-nine thousand dinars!
Twenty-nine!

UNKNOWN MAN (*shouting*): Thirty! I bid thirty thousand dinars!

SLAVE TRADER: Thirty! At a sum of thirty! Thirty thousand
dinars!

SHOEMAKER (*whispering*): Thirty thousand dinars to be thrown into the sea! What a madman!

SLAVE TRADER (*shouting at the top of his voice*): Thirty thousand dinars! Thirty! Any better bid? No one? No one bids more than thirty thousand dinars? Is this all I'm offered as a price for our great Sultan?

SULTAN (*to the Vizier*): So this is the height of noble, patriotic, appreciation!

VIZIER: Your Majesty, those present bidding here are mostly the miserly merchants and well-to-do, those whose nature is niggardly, whose one desire is profit, and who begrudge spending money for the sake of a lofty purpose.

SLAVE TRADER (*shouting*): Thirty thousand dinars! Once again I say: Who bids more? No one? No? No? (*The slave trader exchanges glances with the Vizier, then announces.*) I shall count up to three: One – two – three! That's it! The final price is thirty thousand dinars. (*Cheering from the crowd.*)

WINE MERCHANT (*to the shoemaker*): He's a client of mine, the man who won the auction.

SLAVE TRADER: Come forward the winner! Accept congratulations for your good luck!

The crowds cheer him.

VIZIER: I congratulate you, good citizen, and salute you.

Cheering from the crowd.

SLAVE TRADER (*shouting*): Silence! Silence!

VIZIER (*continuing what he has to say*): I salute you, good citizen, in the name of the fatherland and in the name of this loyal and upright people from whom you have your origins, for buying and ransoming the freedom of our great Sultan. This sublime deed of yours will be inscribed for evermore in the pages of the history of this noble people.

Cheering from the crowd.

SLAVE TRADER (*shouting*): Silence! (*Turns to the unknown man.*) O good citizen, the sum is ready, is it not?

UNKNOWN MAN: Certainly – the sacks of gold are but a few paces away.

SLAVE TRADER: Good. Wait, then, for the venerable Chief Cadi to give his orders.

CADI: The question is decided. The judgement of the law has been carried out. The problem has been solved. Approach, good citizen. Are you able to sign your name?

UNKNOWN MAN: Yes, milord Cadi.

CADI: Sign, then, on these deeds.

UNKNOWN MAN: I hear and obey, milord Cadi.

CADI (*presenting him with a document*): Here – sign here.

UNKNOWN MAN (*reading before signing*): What's this? And that?

CADI: This is the contract of sale.

UNKNOWN MAN: Yes, I'll sign. (*He signs the document.*)

CADI: And this too. (*He presents him with the second document.*)

UNKNOWN MAN: This? What's this?

CADI: This is the deed of manumission.

UNKNOWN MAN (*taking a step backwards*): I'm sorry.

CADI (*taken unawares*): What are you saying?

UNKNOWN MAN: I can't sign this deed.

CADI: Why not? What's this you're saying?

UNKNOWN MAN: I'm saying it's not within my power.

CADI: What's not within your power?

UNKNOWN MAN: To sign the deed of manumission.

CADI (*in a daze*): It's not within your power to sign?

UNKNOWN MAN: No, it's not within my power or authority.

CADI: What's the meaning of this? What do you mean by this? You're undoubtedly mad. It's your bounden duty to sign the deed of manumission. That's the condition – the basic condition for the whole of these proceedings.

UNKNOWN MAN: I much regret that I am in no position to do this. This is beyond me, is outside the limits of my authority.

VIZIER: What's this man saying?

CADI: I don't understand.

VIZIER (*to the unknown man*): Why do you refuse to sign the deed of manumission?

UNKNOWN MAN: Because I have not been given permission to do so.

VIZIER: Have not been given permission?

UNKNOWN MAN (*confirming what he has to say with nods of the head*): I have not been given permission, having been empowered only in respect of the bidding and the contract of sale. Outside this sphere I have no authorization.

CADI: Authorization? Authorization from whom?

UNKNOWN MAN: From the person who appointed me to act for him.

CADI: You are the agent for another person?

UNKNOWN MAN: Yes, milord Cadi.

CADI: Who is this person?

UNKNOWN MAN: I can't say.

CADI: But you must say.

UNKNOWN MAN: No! No, I can't.

VIZIER: You are absolutely required to tell us the person who appointed you to act for him in signing the deed of sale.

UNKNOWN MAN: I cannot divulge his name.

VIZIER: Why?

UNKNOWN MAN: Because I swore an irrevocable oath that I would keep his name a secret.

VIZIER: And why should the person who appointed you be so careful about his name remaining secret?

UNKNOWN MAN: I don't know.

VIZIER: He obviously has a lot of money seeing that he is able to spend this vast sum all at once.

UNKNOWN MAN: These thirty thousand dinars are his whole life's savings.

VIZIER: And he empowered you to put them all into this auction?

UNKNOWN MAN: Yes.

VIZIER: That's the very acme of generosity, the height of noble feeling . . . but why hide his name? Is it modesty? Is it an urgent wish that his bounty should remain hidden and his good deed unknown?

UNKNOWN MAN: Perhaps.

CADI: In such an event he should have given permission to his agent to sign the manumission deed as well.

UNKNOWN MAN: No, he commissioned me to sign only the contract of sale.

CADI: This is evidence of evil intent.

VIZIER: Truly!

SULTAN (*in a sarcastic tone*): It seems that things have become complicated.

CADI: A little, Your Majesty.

VIZIER: This man must speak, otherwise I'll force him to talk.

CADI: Gently, O Vizier, gently. He will talk of his own accord and will answer my questions in friendly fashion. Listen, good man – this person who appointed you, what things does he make in order to earn his living?

UNKNOWN MAN: He makes nothing.

CADI: Has he no trade?

UNKNOWN MAN: They claim he has.

CADI: They claim he has a trade but he does not make anything.

UNKNOWN MAN: That's so.

CADI: Then he's an employee.

UNKNOWN MAN: No.

CADI: He's rich?

UNKNOWN MAN: Fairly so.

CADI: And you're in charge of directing his affairs?

UNKNOWN MAN: That's about it.

CADI: Is he one of the notables?

UNKNOWN MAN: Better than that.

CADI: How's that?

UNKNOWN MAN: The notables visit him but he is unaffected by their visits.

CADI: He's a vizier then?

UNKNOWN MAN: No.

CADI: Has he influence?

UNKNOWN MAN: Yes, on his acquaintances.

CADI: Has he many acquaintances?

UNKNOWN MAN: Yes – many.

CADI (*thinking in silence as he passes his fingers through his beard*): Yes. Yes.

SULTAN: Well finally, O Cadi – have you found a solution to these riddles? Or shall we now spend our time in games of riddles and conundrums?

VIZIER (*his patience exhausted*): We must have resort to the use of force, Your Majesty. There is no other choice open to us. That person, cloaked in secrets and concealing his name, who storms into this auction like this must inevitably be planning some suspiciously dangerous plan of action. With your permission, Your Majesty, I shall act in the matter. (*Calling to the guards.*) Take this man off and torture him till he reveals the name of the person who appointed him and connived with him

UNKNOWN MAN (*shouting*): No! No! No! Don't send me to be tortured! Please! Don't torture me, I implore you!

VIZIER: Then talk!

UNKNOWN MAN: I swore not to.

VIZIER (*to the guards*): Take him away!

The guards surround him.

UNKNOWN MAN: No! No! No!

*The door of the Lady's house is opened. She appears and approaches the
dais, followed by her maid and slave-girls carrying sacks.*

LADY: Leave him! Leave him! It is I who appointed him and
here are your sacks of gold – full thirty thousand dinars in
cash!

Commotion among the crowds.

SLAVE TRADER (*shouting*): Be quiet! Silence!
VIZIER: Who's this woman?
THE CROWDS (*shouting*): The whore whose house is before us.
VIZIER: Whore!
CROWDS: Yes, a whore well known in the district.
SULTAN: Bravo! Bravo! The crowning touch!
VIZIER: You, O woman, are you she who . . .
LADY: Yes, I am the person who authorized this man to take part
in the auction on my account. (*Turning to the unknown man.*) Is
that not so?
UNKNOWN MAN: That's the truth, milady.
VIZIER: You? You dare to buy His Majesty?
LADY: And why not? Am I not a citizen and do I not have
money? Why then should I not have exactly the same rights
as the others?
CADI: Yes, you have this right. The law applies to all. You must
also, however, make yourself acquainted with the conditions
of this sale.
LADY: That's natural. I know it's a sale.
CADI: A sale with a particular characteristic.
LADY: A sale by public auction.
CADI: Yes, but . . .
VIZIER: Before everything else it's a patriotic action. You are a
citizen and I would think you are concerned with the well-
being of the fatherland.
LADY: Without doubt.
VIZIER: Then sign this deed.
LADY: What does this deed contain?
VIZIER: Manumission.
LADY: What does that mean.
VIZIER: Don't you know the meaning of manumission?

LADY: Does it mean giving up what I am in possession of?

VIZIER: Yes.

LADY: Giving up the chattel I bought at the auction?

VIZIER: That's it.

LADY: No, I don't want to give it up.

SULTAN: That's just fine!

VIZIER: You shall give it up, woman!

LADY: No.

VIZIER: Don't force me to be tough. You know that I can force you.

LADY: By what means?

VIZIER (*pointing to his sword*): By this.

SULTAN: Resort to the sword now? The time has passed.

VIZIER: She must yield.

LADY: I do yield, oh Vizier – I yield to the law. Is it not in pursuance of the law that I have signed the contract of sale with the State? Is this law therefore respected or not?

SULTAN: Reply, O Chief Cadi.

CADI: Truly, woman, you have signed a contract of sale but it is a conditional contract.

LADY: Meaning?

CADI: Meaning that it's a sale dependent upon a condition.

LADY: What condition?

CADI: Manumission – otherwise the sale itself becomes null and void.

LADY: You mean, O Cadi, that in order for the sale to become valid I must sign the manumission?

CADI: Yes.

LADY: And you likewise mean that I must sign the manumission so that the purchase may become effective?

CADI: Exactly.

LADY: But, milord Cadi, what is a purchase? Is it not owning a thing in return for a price?

CADI: That is so.

LADY: And what is manumission? Is it not the opposite of possession? Is it not yielding up possession?

CADI: Yes.

LADY: Then, O Cadi, you make manumission a condition of possession, that is to say that in order validly to possess the thing sold, the purchaser must yield up that very thing.

CADI: What? What?

LADY: You're saying, in other words, in order to possess
something you must yield it up.

CADI: What are you saying? In order to possess you must yield
up?

LADY: Or, if you like, in order to possess you must not possess.

CADI: What is this talk?

LADY: This is your condition: in order to buy you must manumit;
in order for me to possess I must not possess. Do you find this
reasonable?

SULTAN: She is right – neither common sense nor logic can accept
this.

CADI: Who taught you this, woman? There is certainly someone
learned in the law, some knowing, impudent debauchee who
has taught her the things she is saying.

SULTAN: What does it matter? That changes nothing. This is *your*
law, O Cadi. Now, you've seen for yourself! With the law
there is always some argument that clashes with some other
argument, and none is devoid of sense and logic.

CADI: But this is picking holes. This is sophistry. What this woman
is saying is mere sophistry.

SULTAN: It's your condition that's sophistry. Selling is selling –
that's self-evident. As for the rest, it is binding on no one.

CADI: Yes, Your Majesty. However, this woman took part in the
auction being aware of the nature of it and knowing full well
the whys and wherefores of it; for her to behave after that
in this way is nothing but trickery, deceit, and double-dealing.

SULTAN: If you now want to give her a lesson in morals, that's
your affair. As for the law, it no longer has a leg to stand on
and you should desist from talking in its name.

CADI: Rather it is my duty, Your Majesty, to protect the law
from such creatures who ridicule and make fun of it.

LADY: I would ask you, O Cadi, not to insult me.

CADI: And you, woman, should be ashamed of yourself – aren't
you embarrassed at this behaviour of yours?

LADY: Embarrassed and ashamed? Why? Because I bought
something the State was selling? Because I refused to be
robbed of the thing I bought, the thing I'd paid such a high
price for? Here are the sacks of gold, count out what is owing
to you and take it!

CADI: I refuse your money, and I thus invalidate this contract.

LADY: For what reason do you invalidate it?

CADI: Because you're a woman of bad reputation and wicked

conduct. This money may well have been earned through immorality, so how can it be accepted as money to be paid to the Exchequer and the State?

LADY: This same money of mine has in fact been accepted as payment for dues and taxes, and are not dues and taxes paid to the Exchequer and the State? If that is your opinion, O Cadi, then I shall not pay a single tax to the State from now on.

SULTAN: Accept her money, O Cadi: it's a lot easier and simpler.

CADI: Then you insist on the stand you've taken, woman?

LADY: Certainly. I am not joking with these sacks of gold. I am paying in order to buy and I buy in order to possess. The law gives me this right. A sale is a sale. Possession is possession. Take your due and hand me over what is mine!

VIZIER: How can you want us to hand over to you the Sultan who rules this land, O woman?

LADY: Why then have you put the Sultan up for sale?

SULTAN: What she says is logical. What a woman!

LADY: I shall reply, for the reply is simple. You put him up for sale so that one of the people might buy him. Now I have bought him, having been the highest bidder at the auction – in public, in front of everyone. Here is the required price and all that remains for you to do is to hand over to me the goods purchased.

SULTAN: The goods?

LADY: Yes, and I demand that they be delivered to the house.

SULTAN: Which house?

LADY: My house of course – this house opposite.

SULTAN (to the Cadi): Do you hear?

CADI: There is no longer any use or point in arguing with a woman of this sort. Your Majesty, I wash my hands of it.

SULTAN: What an excellent solution, Chief Cadi! You land me in this mire and then wash your hands of it.

CADI: I admit my failure – I didn't know I'd be facing this sort of a person.

SULTAN: And then?

CADI: Punish me, Your Majesty. I deserve the most terrible punishment for my bad advice and lack of foresight. Order that my head be cut off!

SULTAN: What's the point of cutting off your head? That head of yours on your shoulders cast me into this plight – will your decapitated head get me out of it?

VIZIER: Leave the matter to me, Your Majesty! I now see clearly
what must be done. (*He draws his sword.*)

SULTAN: No!

VIZIER: But, Your Majesty . . .

SULTAN: I said no. Sheathe your sword!

VIZIER: Listen to me for a moment, Your Majesty.

SULTAN: Sheathe your sword! We have accepted this situation,
so let's proceed.

VIZIER: Your Majesty, seeing that the Cadi has failed and is at a
loss, let us go back to our own methods.

SULTAN: No, I shall not go back.

VIZIER: By the sword everything is easily accomplished and is
solved in the twinkling of an eye.

SULTAN: No, I have chosen the law and I shall continue on that
path whatever obstacles I may encounter.

VIZIER: The law?

SULTAN: Yes, and you yourself said so a while ago and expressed
it in beautiful terms: 'The Sultan has chosen to submit to the
law just like the lowliest individual amongst his subjects.'
These fine words deserve that every effort be expended in
implementing them.

VIZIER: Do you think, Your Majesty, that the lowliest individual
amongst your subjects would agree to accept this situation?
Here are the people standing before us; if you will permit me
I shall ask them and seek their decision. Do you give me
permission?

SULTAN: Do so and show me!

VIZIER (*addressing the crowd*): O people! You see how this
impudent woman treats your august Sultan, are you in
agreement with what she has done?

THE PEOPLE (*shouting*): No!

VIZIER: Are you happy with her insulting behaviour towards our
illustrious ruler?

THE PEOPLE: No!

VIZIER: Do you consider it merits punishment?

THE PEOPLE (*shouting*): Yes!

VIZIER: What is the appropriate punishment for her?

THE PEOPLE (*shouting*): Death!

VIZIER (*turning to the Sultan*): You see, Your Majesty – the people
have given their verdict.

LADY (*turning to the people*): Death for me? Why, O people, do
you condemn me to death? What offence have I committed?

Is buying an affront and a crime? Have I stolen this money?
It is my life's savings. Am I grabbing and making off by
force with the thing offered for sale? I have bought it with
my own money at a public auction before your very eyes. For
what offence do you seek to spill the blood of a weak woman
who has bought something at an auction?

VOICES (*rising from amidst the crowd*): Death to the whore!

OTHER VOICES (*from amongst the crowd*): No, don't kill her!

SULTAN (*to the Vizier*): Do you see?

VIZIER (*to the people*): O people, do you consider that the
judgement against her should be put into effect?

VOICES (*shouting*): Yes!

OTHER VOICES (*shouting*): No!

SULTAN: Opinions are divided, Vizier.

VIZIER: But the majority, Your Majesty, are on the side of death.

SULTAN: For me that is no justification for killing this woman.
You are wanting the excuse of a semi-legal justification for
employing the sword.

VIZIER: The death of this woman is essential for getting us out of
this predicament.

SULTAN: We now need a lifeless corpse to save us?

VIZIER: Yes, Your Majesty.

SULTAN: Once again I am forced to choose between the mire and
blood.

VIZIER: We can no longer force a way out for ourselves other
than by the sword.

SULTAN: He who proceeds forwards along a straight line always
finds a way out.

VIZIER: Your Majesty means . . .

SULTAN: I mean that there is no retreating, no turning back – do
you understand?

VIZIER: I understand, Your Majesty. You wish to go on complying with the law.

SULTAN: Just so, I shall not swerve from what I have chosen, I
shall not go back on what I have decided.

VIZIER: And how shall we go on complying with the law with
which the Cadi himself has announced his defeat and
inability to cope?

SULTAN: He is free to announce his defeat. As for me, I shall not
retreat, so let us proceed along the road to its end.

VIZIER: And this woman who blocks the road for us?

SULTAN: Leave her to me. (*He turns to the woman.*) Come here,

woman! Approach! Another step – here in front of me! I
want to put a few questions to you. Do you permit me?

LADY: I hear and obey, Your Majesty.

SULTAN: First and foremost – who am I?

LADY: Who are you?

SULTAN: Yes, who am I?

LADY: You are the Sultan?

SULTAN: You admit I'm the Sultan?

LADY: Naturally.

SULTAN: Good – and what's the Sultan's job?

LADY: His job is to rule.

SULTAN: You agree that he rules?

LADY: Certainly.

SULTAN: Very good. In as much as you acknowledge all this, how
can you demand that the Sultan be handed over to you?

LADY: Because he has become mine by right.

SULTAN: I do not dispute your right. However, I merely wonder
at the possibility of your implementing this right. In as much
as I am a sultan who rules, how can I carry out the functions
of my office if I am handed over to you in your house?

LADY: Nothing is easier or simpler. You are a sultan during the
day, therefore I shall lend you to the State for the whole of
the day, and in the evening you will return to my house.

SULTAN: I'm afraid you don't understand my work correctly. A
sultan is not the owner of a shop who keeps it open during
the day and then locks it up at night. He is at the beck and
call of the State at any moment. There are urgent and
important questions that often require him to hold talks with
his men of State in the middle of the night.

LADY: This too is an easy matter, for in my house there is a quiet
secluded room where you can work with your men of State.

SULTAN: Do you regard such a set-up as acceptable?

LADY: More than acceptable, I regard it as marvellous!

SULTAN: It is indeed marvellous – a sultan who directs affairs of
State from the house of a woman of whom it is said that she
. . . please forgive me . . . my apologies.

LADY: Say it! Go on! The word no longer wounds me because of
the many torments I have suffered– I have become immune.
However, I assure you, O Sultan, that you will experience
greater joy in my house than you do in yours.

SULTAN: Possibly, except that a ruler is not proficient in carrying out the functions of government when he does so from the houses of others.

LADY: That is if the ruler is free.

SULTAN: You have scored – I am not free. (*He lowers his head. A moment's silence.*)

LADY: What I admire in you, O Sultan, is your composed and calm attitude in the face of this catastrophe.

SULTAN (*raising his head*): You are admitting then that it is a catastrophe?

LADY: It's self-evident – a great Sultan like you being badly treated in this way.

SULTAN: And is anyone but you badly treating me?

LADY: How right you are! What pride and joy it is to me to hear this from the mouth of a great sultan! It's an honour which merits the payment of all the world's gold. No one in the city after today will dare slight me, for I am treating sultans badly!

VIZIER (*in a rage*): Enough, woman! Enough! This is unbearable. She has overstepped all limits of decency. The head of this mischievous and shameless woman must fall!

SULTAN: Calm yourself!

LADY: Yes, calm yourself, O Vizier – and don't interfere in what does not concern you.

VIZIER: How can all this be borne? Patience, Lord! Patience, Lord!

LADY: Yes, have patience, O Vizier, and let the Sultan and me talk. This matter concerns us alone.

SULTAN: That's true.

LADY: Where did we get to, Your Majesty?

SULTAN: I no longer know – it was you who were talking.

LADY: Oh yes, I remember now – we got to where I was saying that it was an honour . . .

SULTAN: For you to treat me badly.

LADY: Rather that I should have the good fortune of enjoying talking to you. In fact, Your Majesty, it's the first time I have seen you at close quarters. People have talked about you so much but I didn't know you were so charming.

SULTAN: Thank you.

LADY: Truly, it's as though we'd been friends for a long time.

SULTAN: Is it your custom to subject your friends to humiliation and ridicule in this manner?

LADY: Not at all – just the opposite.

SULTAN: Then why make an exception of me?

LADY: This in fact is what has begun to upset me. How I would like to bring happiness to your heart and show you reverence and respect! But how? How can I do that! What's the way to do it?

SULTAN: The way's easy.

LADY: By signing this manumission deed?

SULTAN: I would have thought so.

LADY: No, I don't want to let you go. I don't want to give you up. You belong to me. You're mine – mine.

SULTAN: I belong to you and to all the rest of the people.

LADY: I want you to be mine alone.

SULTAN: And my people?

LADY: Your people have not paid gold in order to acquire you.

SULTAN: That's right, but you must know that it's absolutely impossible for me to be yours alone and for me to remain thereafter a sultan. There is only one situation in which it is in order for me to be yours alone.

LADY: What's that?

SULTAN: That I should not be a sultan, that I should give up the throne and relinquish power.

LADY: No, I don't wish that for you– I wish you to remain a sultan.

SULTAN: In that event there must be sacrifice.

LADY: From my side?

SULTAN: Or from my own.

LADY: I should give you up?

SULTAN: Or I should give up the throne?

LADY: It's for me to choose?

SULTAN: Of course it's for you to choose, because all the cards are in your hands.

LADY: Have I all that importance, all that weight?

SULTAN: At this moment, yes.

LADY: This is wonderful!

SULTAN: Certainly.

LADY: Then I now hold all the cards in my hands?

SULTAN: Yes.

LADY: At my pleasure I keep the Sultan in power?

SULTAN: Yes.

LADY: And by a word from me the removal of the Sultan is accomplished?

SULTAN: Yes.

LADY: This is truly wonderful!

SULTAN: Without doubt.

LADY: And who has given me all this authority – money?

SULTAN: The law.

LADY: A word from my mouth can change your destiny and channel your life either to slavery and bondage, or to freedom and sovereignty.

SULTAN: And it is up to you to choose.

LADY (*thoughtfully*): Between bondage that bestows you upon me, and between freedom which retains you for your throne and your people.

SULTAN: It is up to you to choose.

LADY: The choice is difficult.

SULTAN: I know.

LADY: It is painful to let you go, to lose you for ever; but it is also painful to see you lose your throne, for our country has never had the good fortune to have a sultan with such courage and sense of justice. No, do not give up the rule, do not relinquish the throne! I want you to remain a sultan.

SULTAN: And so?

LADY: I shall sign the deed.

SULTAN: The manumission deed?

LADY: Yes.

CADI (*hurrying to present the deed*): Here is the deed.

LADY: I have only a final request.

SULTAN: What is it?

LADY: That you give this night to me, Your Majesty – a single night. Honour me by accepting my invitation and be my guest until daybreak. And when the Muezzin gives the call to dawn prayers from this minaret here, I shall sign the deed of manumission and Your Majesty will be free.

CADI: If the Muezzin does give the call to dawn prayers!

LADY: Yes. Is this too much – that I buy with these sacks of gold not the Sultan himself but a single night with him as my guest?

SULTAN: I accept.

VIZIER: But, Your Majesty, who will guarantee that this promise will be kept by such a woman?

SULTAN: I shall. I am the guarantor, I trust what she says.

CADI: Do you take an oath on what you say, woman?

LADY: Yes, I swear. I swear a triple oath by Almighty God. I

shall sign the deed of manumission when the Muezzin gives
the call to dawn prayers from on top of this minaret.

CADI: I bear witness before God to that. All of us here are
witnesses.

SULTAN: As for me, I believe her without an oath.

LADY: And now, O noble Sultan, will you be so good as to
honour my humble house with your gracious presence?

SULTAN: With great pleasure!

The Sultan rises and follows the lady into her house. Music.

CURTAIN

Act Three

The same square. One side of the mosque with its minaret is in view, also a side of the Lady's house, showing a portion of the room with the window overlooking the square. The time is night. Among the throng are the Vizier, the Shoemaker, and the Wine Merchant.

VIZIER (*in the square, shouting to the guards*): What are all these crowds waiting for in the middle of the night? Turn the people away! Let everyone go to his home, to his bed!

GUARDS (*turning away the crowds*): To your homes! To your houses!

THE CROWDS (*grumbling*): No! No!

SHOEMAKER (*shouting*): I want to stay here.

WINE MERCHANT: And I too shan't budge from here.

VIZIER (*to the guards*): What are they saying?

GUARDS: They refuse to go.

VIZIER (*shouting*): Refuse? What's this nonsense? Make them!

GUARDS (*forcefully*): Everyone to his home! Everyone to his house! Get along! Get along!

SHOEMAKER: I'm already at home. This is my shop.

WINE MERCHANT: I too have my tavern right here before you.

GUARDS: Will you not obey orders? Get going! Get going! (*They push the Wine Merchant and the Shoemaker.*)

SHOEMAKER: There's no reason for violence – please.

WINE MERCHANT: Don't push me about like this!

VIZIER (*to the guards*): Bring along those two trouble-makers! (*The guards seize hold of the Shoemaker and the Wine Merchant and bring them before the Vizier.*)

SHOEMAKER: By God, I haven't done anything, milord Vizier.

VIZIER: Why do you refuse to go home?

SHOEMAKER: I don't want to go to bed. I have a strong desire to stay here, milord Vizier – in order to watch.

VIZIER: To watch what?

SHOEMAKER: To watch Our Majesty the Sultan leaving this house.

WINE MERCHANT: I too, milord Vizier – let me watch it.

VIZIER: Really, what affrontery? Today everyone's affrontery
   has reached the bounds of impudence. Even you and your
   comrade have the nerve to talk in such terms.

WINE MERCHANT: It's not impudence, milord Vizier, it's a
   request.

VIZIER: A request?

SHOEMAKER: Yes, milord Vizier, we request that you give us
   permission to watch.

VIZIER: What insolence! And what have you to do with this
   matter?

SHOEMAKER: Are we not good citizens? The fate of our Sultan
   inevitably concerns us.

VIZIER: This does not give you both the right to disobey orders.

SHOEMAKER: We are not disobeying, we are requesting. How can
   we sleep a wink tonight with the fate of our Sultan in the
   balance?

VIZIER: In the balance?

SHOEMAKER: Yes, milord – the balance of capricious whims.

VIZIER: What do you mean?

SHOEMAKER: I mean that the outcome is not reassuring.

VIZIER: Why do you think so?

SHOEMAKER: With such a woman one can be certain of nothing.

WINE MERCHANT: We have made a bet between ourselves. He
   says this woman will break her promise, while I say she will
   honour it.

VIZIER: A fine thing, indeed – of an important event like this
   you make a game of having bets!

WINE MERCHANT: We are not alone in this, milord Vizier.
   Many such as we among these crowds are tonight making bets
   among themselves. Even the Muezzin and the Executioner
   have made a bet.

VIZIER: The Executioner: where is the Executioner?

WINE MERCHANT (*pointing*): Over there, milord. He's trying to
   hide among the people.

VIZIER (*to the guards*): Bring him over here.
   The guards bring the Executioner to the Vizier.

EXECUTIONER (*frightened*): It's not my fault, milord Vizier. It's
   the Muezzin's mistake. It's he who's responsible, it's he who
   did not give the call to the dawn prayers.

VIZIER: Dawn? What dawn? We're no longer talking about
   dawn prayers, you idiot. (*The Wine Merchant and the Shoemaker
   laugh.*) Do you dare to laugh in my presence? Get out of my

sight! Out! (*The Wine Merchant and the Shoemaker take to their heels.*) And now, Executioner – are you busy with bets?

EXECUTIONER: Bets? Who said so, milord?

VIZIER: I want a straight answer to my question.

EXECUTIONER: But, milord, I . . .

VIZIER: Don't be frightened – tell me.

EXECUTIONER: But this bet, milord . . .

VIZIER: I know, I know, and I shall not punish you. Answer this question frankly: will this woman in your opinion break her promise or will she honour it?

EXECUTIONER: But, milord Vizier, I . . .

VIZIER: I told you not to be frightened but to express your opinion without constraint. That's an order and you must obey it.

EXECUTIONER: Your order must be obeyed, milord – in truth I have no trust in this woman.

VIZIER: Why?

EXECUTIONER: Because she's a liar, a cheat, and a swindler!

VIZIER: Do you know her?

EXECUTIONER: I got to know some of her wiles when I was here that day waiting for the dawn in order to carry out the sentence of execution on the slave trader.

VIZIER: A liar, a cheat, and a swindler?

EXECUTIONER: Yes.

VIZIER: And what does such a woman deserve?

EXECUTIONER: Punishment of course.

VIZIER: And what is the punishment you deem suitable for her if she has tricked and lied to our exalted Sultan?

EXECUTIONER: Death, without doubt!

VIZIER: Good. Then be prepared to carry out this sentence at dawn.

EXECUTIONER (*as though talking to himself*): Dawn? Yet again?

VIZIER: What are you saying?

EXECUTIONER: I am saying that at dawn I shall be ready to execute the order of milord Vizier.

VIZIER: Yes, if the Muezzin has given the call to the dawn prayer and our Sultan has not emerged from this house a free man . . .

EXECUTIONER: Then I cut off the head of this woman.

VIZIER: Yes, as punishment for the crime of . . .

EXECUTIONER: Lying and cheating.

VIZIER: No.

EXECUTIONER (*not understanding*): No?

VIZIER (*as though talking to himself*): No, that is not enough – it is not a crime that merits death. This woman is liable to find some high-sounding phrases in law and logic to justify her action. No, there must be some terrible and serious crime which she will not be able to justify or defend herself against – a crime that will earn her the universal opprobrium of the whole people. We could for instance say she is a spy.

EXECUTIONER: A spy?

VIZIER: Yes, that she's working for the Mongols. Then the people in their entirety will rise up and demand her head.

EXECUTIONER: Yes, an appropriate punishment.

VIZIER: Is that not your opinion?

EXECUTIONER: And I shall raise my voice crying 'Death to the traitor!'

VIZIER: Your voice alone will not suffice. There must be other voices besides yours giving this cry.

EXECUTIONER: There will be other voices.

VIZIER: Do you know whose they'll be?

EXECUTIONER: It won't be difficult to find them.

VIZIER: Witnesses must be got ready.

EXECUTIONER: All that is easy, milord.

VIZIER: I think that such an arrangement can be successful. I'm relying on you if things go badly.

EXECUTIONER: I am your faithful servant, milord Vizier.

A part of the room in the Lady's house is lit up.

VIZIER: Quiet! A light in the window! Let's move away a little.

While the room is lit up, the square becomes dark; the Lady appears and moves towards the sofa followed by the Sultan.

SULTAN (*sitting down*): Your house is magnificent and your furnishings costly.

LADY (*sitting at his feet*): Yes, I told you just now that my husband was a wealthy merchant who had taste and a passion for poetry and singing.

SULTAN: Were you one of his slave-girls?

LADY: Yes, he bought me when I was sixteen years of age, then gave me my freedom and married me several years before his death.

SULTAN: Your luck was better than mine. With you no one forgot to free you at the proper time.

LADY: My real good luck is your having honoured my house with your presence tonight.

SULTAN: Here I am in your house – what do you intend doing with me tonight?

LADY: Nothing except to allow you to relax a little.

SULTAN: Is that all?

LADY: Nothing more than that. Previously I said to you that at my house there is more joy than at yours. I have beautiful slave-girls who excel at dancing and singing and playing on every musical instrument. Be assured, you will not be bored here tonight.

SULTAN: Until dawn breaks?

LADY: Think not of the dawn now. The dawn is still far off.

SULTAN: I shall do all you demand until dawn breaks.

LADY: I shall ask nothing of you except to converse, to take food, and to listen to singing.

SULTAN: Nothing but that?

LADY: But do you want me to ask of you more than that?

SULTAN: I don't know – you know best.

LADY: Let us then start with conversation – tell me about yourself.

SULTAN: About myself?

LADY: Yes, your story – tell me the story of your life.

SULTAN: You want me to tell you stories?

LADY: Yes, in truth you must have a store of wonderfully entertaining stories.

SULTAN: It is *I* now who must tell stories!

LADY: And why not?

SULTAN: Truly that's how it should be, seeing that it is I who am in the position of Shahrazad! She too had to tell stories throughout the whole night, awaiting the dawn that would decide her fate.

LADY (*laughing*): And I, then, am the dreadful, awe-inspiring Shahriyar?

SULTAN: Yes – isn't it extraordinary? Today everything is upside down.

LADY: No, you are always the Sultan. As for me, I am she who plays the role of Shahrazad, always seated at your feet.

SULTAN: A Shahrazad having her apprehensive Shahriyar by the neck until the morning comes.

LADY: No, rather a Shahrazad who will bring joy and gladness to the heart of her sultan. You will see now how I shall deal with your anxiety and misgivings. (*She claps and soothing music issues forth from behind the screens.*)

SULTAN (*after listening for a while*): A delightful performance!

LADY: And I myself shall dance for you. (*She rises and dances.*)

SULTAN (*after she has finished her dance*): Delightful! It's all delightful! Do you do this every night?

LADY: No, Your Majesty. This is an exception. It's just for you, for I myself have not danced since being manumitted and married. On other nights it is the slave-girls who do the dancing and singing.

SULTAN: For your clients?

LADY: My guests, rather.

SULTAN: As you will – your guests. Doubtless these guests of yours pay you a high fee for all this. I now realize how it is you have such wealth.

LADY: My wealth I inherited from my husband. Sometimes I spend on these nights more than I get back.

SULTAN: Why? For nothing?

LADY: For the sake of art. I am a lover of art.

SULTAN (*sarcastically*): Refined art to be sure!

LADY: You don't believe me. You don't take what I say seriously. So be it. Think as badly of me as you like – I am not in the habit of defending myself against other people's assumptions. In people's eyes I am a woman who behaves badly, and I have reached the stage where I have accepted this judgement. I have found this convenient – it is no longer in my interests to correct people's opinion. When one has crossed the ultimate boundaries of wickedness one becomes free, and I am in need of my freedom.

SULTAN: You too?

LADY: Yes, in order to do what I enjoy.

SULTAN: And what do you enjoy?

LADY: The company of men.

SULTAN: Understood!

LADY: No, you understand wrongly. It's not as you think.

SULTAN: How is it then?

LADY: Do you want lies or the truth?

SULTAN: The truth of course.

LADY: You won't believe the truth, so what's the point of my telling it? A truth that people don't believe is a useless truth.

SULTAN: Say it in any case.

LADY: I shall say it purely to amuse you. I enjoy the company of
   men for their souls, not for their bodies. Do you understand?

SULTAN: No, not exactly.

LADY: I shall elucidate. When I was a young slave-girl of the
   same age as the slave-girls I have with me now, my master
   brought me up to love poetry and singing and playing on
   musical instruments. He used to make me attend his banquets
   and converse with his guests, who were poets and singers;
   they also included intellectuals and men of wit and charm.
   We would spend the night reciting poetry, singing and
   playing music and conversing, quoting and capping
   quotations from the masterpieces of literature, and laughing
   from the depths of our hearts. Those were wonderfully
   enjoyable nights, but they were also innocent and chaste.
   Please believe that. My master was a good man and knew no
   pleasure in life other than these nights – a pleasure without
   sin, without vulgarity. In this way did he bring me up and
   educate me. And when I later became his wife he did not wish
   to deprive me of the pleasure of those nights which used so to
   enchant me; he therefore allowed me to continue to attend,
   though from behind silken curtains. That's the whole story.

SULTAN: And after his death?

LADY: After his death I was unable to give up this practice, so I
   continued to invite my husband's guests. At first I would
   receive them screened behind the silken curtains, but when
   the people of the district began spreading gossip at seeing men
   nightly entering the house of a woman with no husband I
   found it pointless to continue to be screened behind the
   curtains. I said to myself: seeing that the people's verdict has
   pronounced me guilty, let me make myself the judge of my
   own behaviour.

SULTAN: It is truly extraordinary that your exterior should
   proclaim so loudly what is not to be found within; your shop
   window advertises goods that are not to be found inside.

LADY: It is for you to believe or not what I have said to you.

SULTAN: I prefer to believe – it is more conducive to peace of
   mind.

LADY: Be that as it may, I do not at all intend to change my life
   and habits. If the road I tread be filled with mire I shall
   continue to wade through it.

SULTAN: Mire! It's to be found on every road– be sure of that!

LADY: Now you remind me of what I did to you in front of the masses of people.

SULTAN: Truly you rolled me in it properly!

LADY: I was intentionally insolent to you, deliberately vulgar and impudent. Do you know why? Because I imagined you as being quite different. I imagined you as an arrogant sultan, strutting about haughtily and giving yourself airs – like most sultans. You could, in fact, well have been even more conceited and overbearing by reason of the wars you have waged and your victories. People always talk of that fabulous ruby which adorns your turban, that ruby that is without peer in the world, of which it is said that you seized it at sword-point from the head of the Mongol Chief. Yes, your deeds are wondrous and splendid. Thus the picture of you in my mind was synonymous with haughtiness, harshness, and cruelty. But as soon as you talked to me so pleasantly and modestly I was overcome by a certain bewilderment and confusion.

SULTAN: Don't be misled! I am not always so pleasant, nor so modest. There are times when I am more cruel and brutal than the worst of sultans.

LADY: I don't believe that.

SULTAN: That's because you've fallen under the influence of the present circumstances.

LADY: You mean that you are specially pleasant to me? This fills me with great pride, dear Majesty. But wait! Perhaps I have misunderstood. What is it that causes you to be so pleasant to me? Is it personal? Or is it the decision you await from me at daybreak?

SULTAN: I affect being pleasant with you, I put it on, in order to gain your sympathy – isn't that so?

LADY: And no sooner will you achieve your freedom than you'll revert to your true nature and will become the cruel Sultan who pursues revenge in order to atone to himself for his moments of humiliation – and then will come my hour of doom.

SULTAN: It would therefore be wise and far-sighted of you to keep me always in your grasp and power.

LADY: Is that so?

SULTAN: That is absolutely logical, seeing that you have your doubts.

LADY: Have I not the right to doubt?

SULTAN: I don't blame you if you do, for it is I who, quite simply and incautiously, have implanted in you the seeds of doubt by saying what I did about myself.

LADY (*regarding him searchingly*): No.

SULTAN: No? Why?

LADY: I prefer to rely on the womanly instinct that is deep within me. It never deceives me.

SULTAN: And what does your womanly instinct tell you?

LADY: It tells me that you are not that type of man. You are different. I should have realized this from the moment I saw you renouncing the use of the sword.

SULTAN: If only you knew how easy things would have been had I used my sword!

LADY: Do you now regret it?

SULTAN: I am merely talking about how easy it would have been. However, the real victory is in solving the problem by sleight-of-hand.

LADY: And this is the path you are now pursuing?

SULTAN: Yes, but I am not confident about the result.

LADY: Let's suppose the result to be that your hopes are dashed – what will you do then?

SULTAN: I have already told you.

LADY: Give up your throne?

SULTAN: Yes.

LADY: No, I do not believe you would really do that. I'm not so simple or stupid as to believe that or to take it seriously. Even if you wanted to do it not a single person in the country would accept it, or would permit you to embark upon such an action. You would bear a heavy burden by accepting the easy solution and would revert to using the simple expedient.

SULTAN: It has never happened that I have taken a step backwards – not even in the field of battle. I admit that this is wrong from the military point of view, for there are circumstances that make retreat necessary. However, I have never done so. Perhaps luck was on my side; in any event I have adopted this bad practice.

LADY: You're amazing!

SULTAN: The truth is rather that I'm an unimaginative man.

LADY: You?

SULTAN: The proof is that were I possessed of imagination and had envisaged what awaited me at the end of such a road, I would have been stunned.

LADY: Nothing stuns you. You have composure, self-confidence, control over your actions, the ability to do what you want with meticulous precision and resoluteness. You are far from being weak or wily – you're frank, natural, and courageous. There's no more to say.

SULTAN: Are you flattering me? Who should be flattering whom? Once again the situations have been reversed.

LADY: Will you permit me, my dear Sultan?

SULTAN: To do what?

LADY: To ask you a personal question?

SULTAN: Personal? Is not all this that we are engaged in personal?

LADY: I want to ask you about – about your heart, about love.

SULTAN: Love? What love?

LADY: Love – for a woman?

SULTAN: Do you imagine I have the time to occupy myself with such things?

LADY: How strange! Has your heart never opened to love a woman?

SULTAN: Why have you opened your large eyes like this in astonishment? Is it such an important matter?

LADY: But you have definitely known many women?

SULTAN: Certainly – that is the nature of military life. The leader of an army, as you know, every night has some female prisoner, some captive, brought to him. Sometimes there are beautiful women among them. That's all there is to it.

LADY: And not a single particular woman succeeded in attracting your glances?

SULTAN: My glances? You should know that at the end of the day I returned always to my tent with eyes filled with the dust of battle.

LADY: And on the following day? Did you not retain a single memory of those beautiful women?

SULTAN: On the following day I would again mount my steed and think of something else.

LADY: But now you're the Sultan. You certainly have sufficient time for love.

SULTAN: Do you believe so?

LADY: What prevents you?

SULTAN: The problems of government. And this is one of them --
  this problem that has descended upon my head today so
  unexpectedly and put me in this fix. Do you consider that
  such a problem allows one to be in the mood for love?

LADY (*laughing*): You're right!

SULTAN: You laugh!

LADY: Another question -- the last, be sure of that! A very
  serious question this time, because it relates to me.

SULTAN: To you?

LADY: Yes. Let us assume that I have manumitted you at dawn --
  you will of course return to your palace.

SULTAN: Of course, I have business awaiting me there.

LADY: And I?

SULTAN: And what about you?

LADY: Will you not think about me after that?

SULTAN: I don't understand.

LADY: You really don't understand what I mean?

SULTAN: You know the language of women is too subtle for me,
  it is very often obscure.

LADY: You understand me only too well, for you are exceedingly
  intelligent and astute, and also very sensitive, despite
  appearances and the impression you like to give. In any case
  I shall explain my words -- here is what I want to know:
  Will you forget me altogether and erase me from your memory
  directly you have left here?

SULTAN: I do not think it is possible to erase you altogether from
  my memory.

LADY: And will you retain a pleasant memory of me?

SULTAN: Certainly!

LADY: Is that all? Does everything for me end just like that?

SULTAN: Are we going over the same ground as before?

LADY: No, I merely wish to ask you: Is this night our last night
  together?

SULTAN: That's a question which it's difficult to answer.

LADY: Good! Don't answer it now!

The maidservant appears.

MAID: Dinner is served, milady.

LADY (*rising to her feet*): If Your Majesty pleases.

SULTAN (*rising to his feet*): You are a model of kindness and
  hospitality.

LADY: Rather is it you who do me a kindness.

She leads him into another room to the accompaniment of music. The light in the house is extinguished and a dim light comes on in the square.

SHOEMAKER (*to the Wine Merchant in a corner of the square*): Look! They've put out the light.

WINE MERCHANT (*looking towards the window*): That's a good sign!

SHOEMAKER: How?

WINE MERCHANT: Putting out the light means going to bed!

SHOEMAKER: And so?

WINE MERCHANT: And so agreement is complete.

SHOEMAKER: Over what?

WINE MERCHANT: Over everything.

SHOEMAKER: You mean that she'll accept to give him up at dawn?

WINE MERCHANT: Yes.

SHOEMAKER: And so you win the bet.

WINE MERCHANT: Without the slightest doubt.

SHOEMAKER: You're over-optimistic, my friend, to think that such a woman would easily accept throwing her money into the sea.

WINE MERCHANT: Who is to know? I say yes.

SHOEMAKER: And I say no.

WINE MERCHANT: Fine, let us await the dawn.

SHOEMAKER: What time is it now?

WINE MERCHANT (*looking at the sky*): According to the stars it is now approximately midnight.

SHOEMAKER: Dawn is still far-off and I am beginning to feel sleepy.

WINE MERCHANT: Go to bed!

SHOEMAKER: I? Out of the question! The whole city is staying up tonight, so how can I be the only one to sleep? In fact I have more reason than anybody to stay up until dawn in order to witness your defeat.

WINE MERCHANT: My defeat?

SHOEMAKER: Without the slightest doubt.

WINE MERCHANT: We shall see which of us turns out to be the loser.

SHOEMAKER (*turning to a corner of the square*): Look! Over there!

WINE MERCHANT: What?

SHOEMAKER (*whispering*): The Vizier and the Executioner. They look as though they're hatching some plot.

WINE MERCHANT: Quiet!

The Vizier walks up and down as he questions the Executioner.

VIZIER: What exactly did you hear from the guards?

EXECUTIONER: I heard them say, milord Vizier, that it was impossible to quell the people and force them to go to bed tonight. The crowds are still standing or squatting in the lanes and alleyways and all are whispering together and gossiping.

VIZIER: Gossiping?

EXECUTIONER: Yes.

VIZIER: And what's all this whispering and gossiping about?

EXECUTIONER: About the business of the Sultan of course and what he's doing tonight in this house.

VIZIER: And what, in your opinion, might he be doing in this house?

EXECUTIONER: Are you asking me, milord Vizier?

VIZIER: Yes, I'm asking you. Are you not one of the people, and does not your opinion represent public opinion? Answer me! What do you imagine the Sultan is doing in this house?

EXECUTIONER: Actually . . . well he's certainly not performing his prayers there!

VIZIER: Are you making fun? Are you being insolent?

EXECUTIONER: Pardon, milord Vizier. I merely wanted to say that this house is not . . . is no saintly place.

VIZIER: Then the gossip in the city is along these lines – that the Sultan is spending the night in a . . .

EXECUTIONER: A brothel!

VIZIER: What are you saying?

EXECUTIONER: That's what they are saying, milord. I am reporting what I heard.

VIZIER: Is this all that people are mentioning about this important matter? They are forgetting the noble purport, the lofty aim, the sublime concept, the patriotic objective! Even you, as I see it, have forgotten all this.

EXECUTIONER: No, milord Vizier, I have forgotten nothing.

VIZIER: We shall see. Tell me then why the Sultan accepted to enter this house.

EXECUTIONER: In order to . . . to gratify the whore.

VIZIER: Is that all it's about? What a shallow way of looking at things!

EXECUTIONER: Milord Vizier, I was present and I saw and heard everything from the beginning.

VIZIER: And you didn't understand any of it, except for the insignificant and degrading side of the issue. Are there many like you among the people?

EXECUTIONER: Like me they were all present.

VIZIER: And they all made of it what you did as far as I can see. Their talk does not deal with the profound reason, the exalted meaning of all that has happened. Their talk deals merely with what you yourself say: the Sultan is spending the night in a brothel! What a catastrophe! It's this that's the real catastrophe!

The Chief Cadi appears.

CADI: I haven't slept tonight.

VIZIER: You too?

CADI: Why I too?

VIZIER: The whole of the rest of the city hasn't slept tonight.

CADI: I know that.

VIZIER: And everyone's whispering and gossiping.

CADI: I know that as well.

VIZIER: And do you know what they're saying in the city?

CADI: The worst possible things. The point of interest and excitement for the people is the scandalous side of the affair.

VIZIER: Unfortunately so.

CADI: It's my fault.

VIZIER: And mine too. I should have been more resolute in the defence of my opinion.

CADI: But, on the other hand, how could we have anticipated that woman's intervention?

VIZIER: We should have anticipated everything.

CADI: You're right.

VIZIER: Now the die is cast and we have no power to do anything.

CADI: Yet it is in our power to snatch the Sultan away from this house.

VIZIER: We must wait for the dawn.

CADI: No, now . . . at once!

VIZIER: But the dawn is still far off.

CADI: It must be made to come now – at once!

VIZIER: Who? What?

CADI: The dawn!

VIZIER: My apologies – I don't understand.

CADI: You will shortly. Where's the Muezzin of this mosque?

VIZIER (*turning towards the Executioner*): The Executioner must know.

EXECUTIONER: He's over there, among the crowds.

CADI: Go and bring him to me.

The Executioner returns, and after some whispered conversation hurries off obediently.

VIZIER (*to the Cadi*): It seems you have some plan or other?

CADI: Yes.

VIZIER: May I know it?

CADI: Shortly.

The Muezzin appears, panting.

MUEZZIN: Here I am, milord Cadi.

CADI: Come close! I want to talk to you regarding the dawn.

MUEZZIN: The dawn? Be sure, milord Cadi, that I have committed no wrong. This Executioner is accusing me falsely of . . .

CADI: Listen to me well.

MUEZZIN: I swear to you, milord Cadi, that on that day . . .

CADI: Will you stop this nonsensical chattering! I told you to listen to me well. I want you to carry out what I am going to say to the letter. Do you understand?

MUEZZIN: Yes.

CADI: Go and climb up into your minaret and give the call to the dawn prayer.

MUEZZIN: When?

CADI: Now!

MUEZZIN (*in surprise*): Now?

CADI: Yes, immediately.

MUEZZIN: The dawn prayer?

CADI: Yes, the dawn prayer. Go and give the call to the dawn prayer. Is what I say clear or not?

MUEZZIN: It's clear, but it's now approximately . . . midnight.

CADI: Let it be!

MUEZZIN: Dawn at midnight?

CADI: Yes! Hurry!

MUEZZIN: Isn't this just a little . . . premature?

CADI: No.

MUEZZIN (*whispering to himself*): I'm at a loss about this dawn – sometimes I'm asked to put it back and sometimes I'm asked to bring it forward.

CADI: What are you saying?

MUEZZIN: Nothing, milord Cadi. I shall go at once to carry out your order.

CADI: Listen! Make sure you tell no one that it was the Cadi who gave you this order.

MUEZZIN: Meaning, milord?

CADI: Meaning that it's you on your own initiative who have acted thus.

MUEZZIN: On my own initiative? I go up into the minaret to give the call to dawn prayers at midnight? Anyone behaving like that *must* be a crazy idiot.

CADI: Leave to me the task of explaining your behaviour at the appropriate time.

MUEZZIN: But, milord, by this action I expose myself to the ridicule of the masses and they'll ask that I be punished.

CADI: And whom will you appear before to be tried? Won't it be before me, the Chief Cadi?

MUEZZIN: And if you disown and abandon me?

CADI: Do not be afraid, that will never happen.

MUEZZIN: And how can I be sure?

CADI: I promise you – have you no faith in my promise?

MUEZZIN (*whispering to himself*): The promises tonight are many – and not a soul is sure of anything.

CADI: What are you saying?

MUEZZIN: Nothing. I'm just asking myself – why should I expose myself to all this danger?

CADI: It's a service you're rendering the State.

MUEZZIN (*in astonishment*): The State?

CADI: Yes, I shall tell you about the matter so that you may rest assured. Listen! If you give the call to dawn prayers now, the Sultan will immediately leave this house a free man. That, in a couple of words, is what it's all about. Do you understand now?

MUEZZIN: It's a patriotic act!

CADI: It certainly is. What do you say then?

MUEZZIN: I shall do it immediately. I shall be proud of it the whole of my life. Permit me, milord Cadi, also to tell you something – what I say being strictly between ourselves – which is that I previously told you a small falsehood of this sort in order to save the head of someone who had been condemned to death; so why should I not commit a similar falsehood in order to gain the freedom of Our Majesty the beloved Sultan!

CADI: You're quite right, but I enjoin you to secrecy. Be careful not to let that tongue of yours wag! Hide this pride of yours in your soul, for if you begin to boast of what you have done in these present circumstances the whole business will be ruined. Shut your mouth well if you want your action to bear fruit and be appreciated.

MUEZZIN: I shall shut my mouth.

CADI: Good. Hurry off and do it.

MUEZZIN: As swift as the winds I'll be!

The Muezzin leaves hurriedly.

CADI (*to the Vizier*): What do you think?

VIZIER: Do you think a trick like this will put matters right?

CADI: Yes, in the best way possible. Tonight I set about considering every aspect of the matter. I no longer regard myself as having been defeated. I still have in my quiver – or, to be more exact, in the law's quiver – many tricks.

VIZIER: Let us pray to God to make your tricks successful this time. Your personal honour is at stake.

CADI: You will see.

The voice of the Muezzin rings out.

MUEZZIN (*from afar*): God is great! God is great! Come to prayers! Come to prayers! Come to salvation! Come to salvation!

The crowd make their appearance in a state of agitation, astonishment, protest, and anger.

THE PEOPLE (*shouting*): The dawn? Now? It's still night – we're

in the middle of the night. He's mad! This madman – arrest
him! Bring him down, bring him down from on top of the
minaret! Bring him down!

VIZIER (*to the Cadi*): The crowds will fall upon this poor fellow.

CADI: Order your guards to disperse the crowds.

VIZIER (*shouting at the guards*): Clear the square! Clear everyone
out of the square!

*The guards chase the people away and clear the square, while the
Muezzin continues with his call to prayer.*

*The light goes on in the Lady's room. She appears at the window
followed by the Sultan.*

LADY: Is it really dawn?

CADI: It is the call to prayers. Come down here at once!

LADY: This is absurd – look at the stars in the sky.

SULTAN (*looking at the sky*): Truly this is most strange.

CADI (*to the Lady*): I told you to come down here immediately.

SULTAN (*to the Lady*): Let us go down together to see what it's all
about.

LADY: Let us go, Your Majesty. (*They leave the room, the light is
extinguished, and they are seen coming out of the house.*)

SULTAN (*looking at the sky*): The dawn? At this hour?

VIZIER: Yes, Your Majesty.

SULTAN: This is truly extraordinary. What do you say, Cadi?

CADI: No, Your Majesty, the dawn has not yet broken.

VIZIER (*taken aback*): How's that?

CADI: It's quite obvious – it's still night.

VIZIER (*to the Cadi in astonishment*): But . . .

CADI: But we have all heard the Muezzin give the call to dawn
prayers. Did you hear it, woman?

LADY: Yes, I did.

CADI: You admit then that you heard the voice of the Muezzin
giving the call to dawn prayers?

LADY: Yes, but . . .

CADI: There is nothing more to be said. As you have admitted
this, there is nothing left for you to do but keep your promise.
Here is the deed of manumission – you have only to sign.

He presents her with the deed.

LADY: I promised to sign it at dawn and here you are admitting, O Cadi, that it's still night.

CADI: Not so fast, woman! Your promise is inscribed in my head, word for word. Your exact words were: 'When the Muezzin gives the call to dawn prayers.' The whole matter now comes down to this question: have you or have you not heard the voice of the Muezzin?

LADY: I heard it, but if the dawn's still far off . . .

CADI: The dawn as such is not in question – the promise related to the voice of the Muezzin as he gave the call to the dawn prayer. If the Muezzin has made a mistake in his calculation or conduct, it is he who is responsible for his mistake – that's his business. It's not ours. You understand?

LADY: I understand – it's not a bad trick!

CADI: The Muezzin will of course be prosecuted for his mistake. This, however, doesn't change the facts, which are that we have all heard the Muezzin giving the call to the dawn prayers from on top of his minaret. And so all the legal consequences deriving therefrom must take their course – immediately! Come along then and sign!

LADY: Is it thus that you interpret my one condition before manumitting the Sultan?

CADI: In the same manner as you interpreted our condition when you purchased the Sultan!

VIZIER: You have fallen into the very same snares of the law. Therefore, submit and sign!

LADY: This is not honest! It's sheer trickery!

VIZIER: Trickery matched by trickery! You began it – and he who begins is the greater offender. You are the last person to object and protest.

SULTAN (shouting): Shame! Enough! Enough! Stop this nonsense! Cease this pettiness! She shall not sign. I absolutely refuse that she should sign this way. And you, Chief Cadi, aren't you ashamed of yourself for fooling around with the law like this?

CADI: Milord Sultan . . .

SULTAN: I am disappointed. I am disappointed in you, Chief Cadi. Is this, in your opinion, the law? The expenditure of effort and skill in trickery and fraud!

CADI: Your Majesty, I merely wanted . . .

SULTAN: To rescue me, I know that, but did you think I'd accept being rescued by such methods?

CADI: With such a woman, Your Majesty, we have the right . . .

SULTAN: No, you have no right at all to do this. You have no such right. Maybe it was the right of this woman to indulge in trickery – she cannot be blamed if she did so; maybe she should be the object of indulgence because of her intelligence and skill. As for the Chief Cadi, the representative of justice, the defender of the sanctity of the law, the upright servant of the canonical law, it is one of his most bounden duties to preserve the law's purity, integrity, and majesty, whatever the price. It was you yourself who first showed me the virtue of the law and the respect it must be shown, who told me that it was the supreme power before which I myself must bow. And I have bowed down right to the end in all humility. But did it ever occur to me that I would see you yourself eventually regarding the law in this manner; stripping it of its robe of sanctity so that it becomes in your hands no more than wiles, clauses, words – a mere plaything?

CADI: Let me explain to you, Your Majesty . . .

SULTAN: No, explain nothing. Go now! It's better for you to go home and betake yourself to bed until the morning. As for me I shall respect this lady's situation – in the true sense in which we all understand it. Let us go, milady! Let us return to your house! I am at your disposal.

LADY: No, Your Majesty.

SULTAN: No?

LADY: No, your Chief Cadi wanted to rescue you, and I don't want to be any less loyal than him towards you. You are now free, Your Majesty.

SULTAN: Free?

LADY: Yes, bring the deed of manumission, Chief Cadi, so that I may sign it.

CADI: You'll sign it now?

LADY: Yes, now.

CADI (*presenting her with the deed*): God grant she's telling the truth!

LADY (*signing the deed*): Believe me this time! There's my signature!

CADI (*examining the signature*): Yes, despite everything you're a good woman.

SULTAN: Rather is she one of the most outstanding of women! The people of the city must respect her. That's an order, O Vizier!

VIZIER: I hear and obey, Your Majesty!

CADI (*folding up the deed*): Everything has now been completed, Your Majesty, in first-class fashion.

SULTAN: And without a drop of blood being spilt – that's the important thing.

VIZIER: Thanks to your courage, Your Majesty. Who would imagine that to proceed to the end of this road would require more courage than that of the sword?

CADI: Truly!

SULTAN: Let us give praise to the generosity of this noble lady. Allow me, milady, to address my thanks to you, and I ask that you accept the return of your money to you, for there is no longer any reason why you should lose it. Vizier! Pay her from my private purse the amount which she has lost.

LADY: No, no, Your Majesty. Don't take away this honour from me. There are no riches in the world, in my opinion, to equal this beautiful memory on which I shall live for the whole of my life. With something so paltry I have participated in one of the greatest of events.

SULTAN: Good – as the memory has such significance for you, then keep this memento of it. (*He takes the enormous ruby from his turban.*)

VIZIER (*whispering*): The ruby? The one without peer in the world?

SULTAN: Compared with your goodness, this is accounted a petty thing.

(*He presents her with the ruby.*)

LADY: No, dear Majesty, I don't deserve, am not worthy of this . . . this . . .

SULTAN (*starting to leave*): Farewell, good lady!

LADY (*with tears in her eyes*): Farewell, dear Sultan!

SULTAN (*noticing her tears*): Are you crying?

LADY: With joy!

SULTAN: I shall never forget that I was your slave for a night.

LADY: For the sake of principles and the law, Your Majesty! (*She lowers her head to hide her tears.*)

Music. The Sultan's cortège moves off.

CURTAIN

Not a Thing out of Place

Characters
BARBER
CUSTOMER
POSTMAN
YOUNG MAN (*in European dress*)
YOUNG LADY
MAN WITH TWIRLED MOUSTACHES (*in European dress*)
VILLAGERS

Not a Thing out of Place

A village square near the station. A barber has set up by a wall; he has a customer and is sharpening his razor.

BARBER (*taking hold of the customer's bald head*): When there's a water-melon right there in front of you all nice and shiny, how can you find out whether it's red inside or unripe except by splitting it open with a knife?

CUSTOMER (*disturbed*): What's the connection?

BARBER: Nothing at all, just that certain things remind one of others.

CUSTOMER: What things? What reminds you?

BARBER: Tell me, can you know what's inside this head of yours?

CUSTOMER: What are you getting at? Do you mean in the way of ideas?

BARBER: What ideas are you talking about, man? Who mentioned ideas? We're talking about water-melons.

CUSTOMER: I don't get it at all.

BARBER: Just let me explain. It's something that can be perfectly well understood. If you've got a water-melon in your hand, what do you do with it? Play football with it?

CUSTOMER: Of course not.

BARBER: Quite so. That's just what happened – my brother wasn't wrong then.

CUSTOMER: Your brother?

BARBER: Yes, my full brother. God bless him, he was a real fine barber like myself.

CUSTOMER: What about the water-melon?

BARBER: A customer's head – and not a wit better than that of your good self.

CUSTOMER (*with a cry of alarm*): Customer's head?

BARBER: And so what? Slice it.

CUSTOMER: What do you mean 'so what'? Slice the customer's head?

BARBER: Isn't that the way to see whether it's red inside or unripe?

CUSTOMER (*looking in fear at the razor*): With a razor?

BARBER: You see, at the time he happened to have the razor in his hand and the soap was on the customer's chin.

CUSTOMER (*fearfully*): And what happened after that?

BARBER: I swear to you, they carted him off to hospital.

CUSTOMER: The customer?

BARBER: My brother.

CUSTOMER: Your brother? It was *he* they carted off? But why?

BARBER: What d'you think they said? They said he was mad. Can you believe it? Can you credit it?

CUSTOMER: I really can't. So they carted him off to the lunatic asylum?

BARBER: That's right, sir. Can you imagine such a thing?

CUSTOMER: And the customer?

BARBER: He was carted off by ambulance.

CUSTOMER: God Almighty! The good Lord preserve us!

BARBER (*sharpening his razor on the palm of his hand*): Just put yourself in my brother's place. In front of you there's a water-melon and you're holding a knife. What would you do?

CUSTOMER: And have you ever done it?

BARBER: God be my witness – up until now, no.

CUSTOMER: Any intention of doing so?

BARBER: Maybe. After all, is there anything wrong about slicing a water-melon with a razor?

CUSTOMER (*tearing the towel from his neck*): I'm off!

BARBER: Where to? There's still the other side to be done.

CUSTOMER: One side's quite enough. 'Bye. (*The customer makes his escape at a run.*)

A postman appears carrying a handful of letters.

POSTMAN: What's that customer of yours running off for with the soap still on his chin?

BARBER: Mad, God spare you.

POSTMAN (*holding out the handful of letters*): Take delivery of today's post.

BARBER: Just throw them down in the old basin as usual.

POSTMAN (*hands him the letters*): Take them and throw them in yourself, then come along and let's have a game.

BARBER (*taking the letters and throwing them down into a nearby basin on the floor*): What shall we play today?

A young man in European dress appears.

YOUNG MAN (*to the postman*): Is there a letter for me? My name's . . .

POSTMAN (*interrupting him*): There are plenty of letters for you. Just choose yourself the letter you fancy.

YOUNG MAN: But I want a letter addressed to me.

POSTMAN: Are you new to the village?

YOUNG MAN: I arrived here only yesterday. I came for my cousin's wedding.

POSTMAN: You don't know how naïve you're being. In this village, son, we don't have the time to deliver letters to people. The whole postbag's in the basket . . .

BARBER: In the basin . . .

POSTMAN: In the master barber's basin – and what a blessed and auspicious basin it is! Everyone comes along and simply takes his pick – be it addressed to him, to someone else, it's no concern of ours. The great thing is to get rid of the post day by day.

YOUNG MAN: You mean you take a letter that doesn't belong to you?

POSTMAN: One letter, two – just as your fancy takes you.

YOUNG MAN: My fancy? What's my fancy to do with it? I want a letter that's mine.

POSTMAN: Every letter you have here is yours. Open any letter and you'll find it contains amusing things. Don't you want to be amused?

YOUNG MAN: Whatever are you saying? Is this how you're dealing with people's letters?

POSTMAN: Every day – and the people like it this way. In a couple of hours they've swiped the lot.

YOUNG MAN: But this is what's called chaos.

POSTMAN: Not at all. That chaos you're talking about is something altogether different.

BARBER: That sort of chaos doesn't happen here, my dear sir – thank God! Like me to give you a shave?

YOUNG MAN: No thanks, I've just shaved.

BARBER: I'll crop a bit of the fur off the water-melon?

YOUNG MAN: Water-melon?

POSTMAN: What he means, begging your pardon, is that he'll shave your head for you.

YOUNG MAN: No – thanks.

POSTMAN: Then grab yourself a couple of letters from the basin and take yourself off. The fact is we just haven't got the time.

YOUNG MAN (*goes up to the basin and searches for a letter addressed to him*): No letters for me. 'Bye. (*He is about to depart.*)

POSTMAN (*stopping him*): Going away empty-handed like that? Man, take yourself a letter from those in front of you. Like me to choose you one? (*He goes up to the basin and chooses a letter.*) Take this one – it's in a woman's handwriting. You'll enjoy it.

YOUNG MAN (*hesitating*): Yes, but . . .

POSTMAN: But what? Don't say 'but'. Go on – don't embarrass me. Really, don't embarrass me.

BARBER: Go on and take it. Don't embarrass him. Put your trust in God and off you go. We just haven't got the time to attend to you.

YOUNG MAN (*takes the letter from the postman*): Hope it's all right! What an extraordinary thing!

He goes off with the letter.

POSTMAN: What were we talking about before that asinine young fellow came along?

BARBER: We were saying what would we play today.

POSTMAN: Yes, quite right – what shall we play? I'll tell you what – we'll play the game of the donkey and the philosopher.

BARBER: What's a philosopher?

POSTMAN: Someone with a big brain.

BARBER: That'll be me.

POSTMAN: No, you're the donkey.

BARBER: Why?

POSTMAN: Because a donkey's got a bigger brain.

BARBER: How's that?

POSTMAN: I'll tell you: Ever seen a donkey having a shave at a barber's?

BARBER: No.

POSTMAN: Is that clever of him or not?

BARBER: Yes.

POSTMAN: Right, then I'll be the donkey.

BARBER: Just now you said I'd be the donkey.

POSTMAN: I've changed my mind.

BARBER: What about me – who'll I be?

POSTMAN: You'll be the philosopher.

BARBER: No thanks, I don't want to be no philosopher.

POSTMAN: You silly man, a philosopher's more intelligent.

BARBER: Do you take me for a fool? Do you think I'm so gaga I don't know?

POSTMAN: Don't you believe me? All right, go and ask anyone: Is a donkey more intelligent than a philosopher? He'll tell you . . .

BARBER: I'll tell you myself. Ever seen a donkey going off to post a letter?

POSTMAN: No.

BARBER: Is that intelligent or not?

POSTMAN: Yes.

BARBER: Right, then I'll be the donkey.

POSTMAN: But, my dear fellow, I want to be the donkey.

BARBER: You be a donkey as well – then we'll both be donkeys. What's wrong with that?

POSTMAN: It's no good, one of us must be a philosopher. That's how the game's played.

BARBER: I'm no good for a philosopher – I've got a big brain.

POSTMAN: And I'm the empty-headed one?

BARBER: No, not at all, I just meant that. . . .

The young man reappears, the opened letter in his hand.

YOUNG MAN: This letter's from a girl to her fiancé. She tells him to meet her off the noon train.

POSTMAN: There's the noon train giving a whistle – it's inside the station.

YOUNG MAN: What's to be done now?

POSTMAN: Very simple – go and meet her at the station.

YOUNG MAN: Who shall I meet?

POSTMAN: Man, the girl who sent you the letter.

YOUNG MAN: She didn't send it to me.

POSTMAN: Isn't that it in your hand?

YOUNG MAN: But it isn't for me, it isn't mine.

POSTMAN: What did you open it for then?

YOUNG MAN: You handed it to me.

POSTMAN: And you took it and opened it and read it. It's therefore yours. Off you go and meet the lady at the station.

YOUNG MAN: And how shall I recognize her?

POSTMAN: You'll recognize her all right if she's pretty.

YOUNG MAN: Pretty?

POSTMAN: Pretty and on her own and getting off the train looking to right and left.

BARBER (*to the young man*): Man, go and meet her. Don't be so gormless.

YOUNG MAN: How extraordinary! Hope it's all right! (*He goes off in the direction of the station.*)

POSTMAN: Now take this young fellow: Is he a donkey or a philosopher?

BARBER: If he gets off with the lady he'll be a donkey.

POSTMAN: He'll be a philosopher, fool!

BARBER: How's that?

The customer, half his face in lather, reappears.

CUSTOMER: D'you like the idea of me walking around half shaved?

BARBER: Is that my fault? – it's you who ran off like a madman.

CUSTOMER: So it's I who's mad?

BARBER: Well, I then?

CUSTOMER: And what about your brother – you well know the one I mean?

BARBER: And what about my brother?

CUSTOMER: The water-melon . . .

BARBER: Man, have some sense – is this the season for water-melons?

CUSTOMER: Thanks be to God – you've put my mind at rest. So you had no intention . . .

BARBER: To do what?

CUSTOMER: To slice the water-melon?

BARBER: Man, talk sense, can't you. Where's this water-melon you're talking of?

CUSTOMER: My head.

BARBER: This head of yours a water-melon?

CUSTOMER: You mean it's not a water-melon?

BARBER: You asking me?

CUSTOMER: Then what you said was a joke?

BARBER: What d'you mean 'joke', man? Why should I joke with customers? All I say is dead serious.

CUSTOMER: You mean then that the story of the water-melon was serious?

BARBER: Of course it was serious.

CUSTOMER: Meaning that you were seriously intending to slice the water-melon?

BARBER: D'you think I was going to play football with it or just sit down and look at it?

CUSTOMER: Good God! 'Bye. (*He makes off hurriedly.*)

BARBER: Why's he run away again? What would you say about him too – a philosopher or a donkey?

POSTMAN: It seems there are a lot of philosophers around these days.

BARBER: Then why not ask him to play with us?

POSTMAN: A stranger wouldn't fit in with us.

BARBER (*looking in the direction of the station*): Good heavens! Just look – the young fellow's coming along with the lady.

POSTMAN: She must have turned out to be pretty!

The young man and the lady – a young and beautiful girl – approach. He is carrying her suitcase for her.

YOUNG LADY: But where is he? Why wasn't he waiting for me at the station?

YOUNG MAN: After all, *I* was waiting for you.

YOUNG LADY: But you're not he.

YOUNG MAN: Who am I then?

YOUNG LADY: How should I know who you might be?

YOUNG MAN: How don't you know – wasn't it you who wrote this letter and posted it to me? (*He shows her the letter.*)

YOUNG LADY: Yes, it was I who wrote and posted it, but . . .

YOUNG MAN: Fine, then I'm he.

YOUNG LADY: But you're not he.

YOUNG MAN: Was he old?

YOUNG LADY: No, young.

YOUNG MAN: And what am I – old or young?

YOUNG LADY: Young of course.

YOUNG MAN: That settles it – I'm he.

YOUNG LADY: How do you work that out?

YOUNG MAN: Don't you believe me? Come along and we'll ask some of the locals. (*He moves towards the postman and the barber.*) Please tell us, gentlemen: am I he or not?

POSTMAN: You are.

BARBER: The very same.

YOUNG MAN: You've heard for yourself.

YOUNG LADY: That's crazy talk.

POSTMAN: Tomorrow you'll come to your senses.

BARBER: In the same way as the gentleman has. (*He points at the young man.*)

YOUNG MAN (*to the young lady*): The most important people in the village have ruled that I am he – so I *am* he. Come on, let's go off to the registrar.

YOUNG LADY: Registrar?

YOUNG MAN: Of course. Aren't we engaged to be married? All that remains therefore is the registrar.

YOUNG LADY: But that's impossible.

YOUNG MAN: Why impossible? Everything's possible.

YOUNG LADY: Hey – and what about my fiancé?

YOUNG MAN: But, my dear lady, I'm your fiancé. It's I who received your letter and it was I who met you at the station. The villagers have borne witness to it.

YOUNG LADY: What an odd sort of village this is!

YOUNG MAN: What's wrong with this village? It's the very best; it's the one you arrived at to meet up with your fiancé and – Allah be praised – I've done just that.

YOUNG LADY: But that's absolutely impossible.

YOUNG MAN: Only too possible. Everything's possible here.

YOUNG LADY: But it's not reasonable.

YOUNG MAN: Everything's reasonable here. God be my witness – I am now absolutely convinced.

POSTMAN: Convinced that this village of ours is not chaotic?

YOUNG MAN: Absolutely so – in this place of yours not a thing is out of place.

BARBER: Put your trust in God then and off you go to the registrar's.

YOUNG MAN: And the village registrar, is he like your good selves, with never a thing out of place?

BARBER: Have no fear – put a summer water-melon in your stomach and relax!

POSTMAN: Let's do without the water-melon – this is not the place for it!

YOUNG MAN: What are you driving at?

POSTMAN: Relax – we're talking about some other water-melon.

YOUNG MAN: Then you're agreed about our being engaged and going off to the registrar's?

BARBER: Agreed.

POSTMAN: Absolutely agreed.

YOUNG LADY: But I'm not agreed.

YOUNG MAN: That's something to be said in front of the registrar – he'll deal with it.

YOUNG LADY: How'll he deal with it?

YOUNG MAN: Just as our good friend the postman dealt with matters – and he did so very soundly.

YOUNG LADY: It's extraordinary!

YOUNG MAN: I said that before you did. Come on, let's go off to the registrar's.

YOUNG LADY: Heaven knows how all this is going to end! (*The young man leads her away by the hand.*)

POSTMAN: The end will be like the beginning – all one and the same!

BARBER: And half a shave's like a whole one – all one and the same!

POSTMAN: And a letter of yours turns out not to be yours – all one and the same!

BARBER: And a head you think is a water-melon, and a water-melon you think is a head – all one and the same!

POSTMAN: And where the village registrar is concerned . . .

BARBER: All's one and the same.

POSTMAN: Let's give them a send-off.

BARBER: Bring the drum!

POSTMAN: Where's the flute?

BARBER: And let the village folk gather round – they're great ones for fun and gaiety.

POSTMAN: Yes, they never miss a chance for making merry. Go on, give them a call!

BARBER (*together with the postman he calls out*): Villagers! Villagers! Bring your drums and flutes! (*Some of the villagers begin to gather together.*)

A man in European dress with twirled moustaches appears.

MAN IN EUROPEAN DRESS: What's happening around here? Why are you calling to the villagers?

POSTMAN: What's it to you?

MAN IN EUROPEAN DRESS: What are you talking to me like that for?

BARBER: And who twirled your moustaches like that for you? What d'you reckon to have standing on them?

MAN IN EUROPEAN DRESS: And what are you being so rude for?

BARBER: And if I'm rude, who d'you think you are?

MAN IN EUROPEAN DRESS: And why would you be asking me that?

POSTMAN: In order to learn the reason for your honouring this place with your presence.

MAN IN EUROPEAN DRESS: And you still don't know why I'm here in this village?

POSTMAN: No, why?

MAN IN EUROPEAN DRESS: Why?

BARBER: Yes, why?

MAN IN EUROPEAN DRESS: I'm an Inspector . . .

POSTMAN (in alarm): Good God! We're in a real mess now! You're an Inspector? A Police Inspector?

MAN IN EUROPEAN DRESS: No . . .

BARBER: A Special Branch Inspector?

MAN IN EUROPEAN DRESS: An Inspector of Music in the band of the world-famous singer Nabawiya Santawiya, otherwise known far and wide as Naboubou!

BARBER: The Devil take you far and wide! You scared the life out of us.

POSTMAN: Yes, why didn't you say so right from the beginning? And what brought you here?

MAN IN EUROPEAN DRESS: We came for a wedding feast being held in the village.

BARBER: It must be the wedding of that fellow over there with the young lady.

POSTMAN: We were just about to give them a send-off.

MAN IN EUROPEAN DRESS: Why, are you two working in Madame Shakaa Bakaa's band?

BARBER: Shakaa Bakaa?

MAN IN EUROPEAN DRESS: That dead-beat singer who's competing with us wherever we go.

POSTMAN: No, sir, we don't work in any band.

MAN IN EUROPEAN DRESS: Amateurs?

BARBER: No, sir, we're respectable and sensible people. My honoured friend is the Grand Bey, Director of the District Post Office, while I myself am the owner of the hairdressing establishments in the district.

MAN IN EUROPEAN DRESS (looking at the corner of the barber's stall

and the basinful of letters): Just the place for them! Honoured
to have made your acquaintance.

POSTMAN: Come on, let's give the young man and his lady a real
send-off all the way up to the registrar's! Villagers! Villagers!
Where are your drums? Where your flutes? Where the
dancers among you?

*The people of the village gather together with excited shouting, with
singing and mad dancing, while chanting.*

> *Dancing to sound of drum and flute*
> *Into reverse the world we'll put –*
> *And yet it's going right we'll find.*
> *Whether sane or out of mind*
> *It really matters not at all.*
> *Come step it out now, one and all.*

CURTAIN